# The Old Farmhouse Kitchen

## RECIPES AND OLD-TIME NOSTALGIA

### BY FRANCES A. GILLETTE
### PHOTOGRAPHY BY GABRIELLE MASSIE

**TYPING BY Brooke Tormanen**
**Krista Kaski**

**EDITED AND PUBLISHED BY Frances A. Gillette**

**LAYOUT BY Infinite Color, Inc.**
**Ward Homola**
*www.infinitecolor.com*

**PRINT PRODUCTION BY WestCoast PrintShop**
**Mike Williamson**
*www.westcoastprintshop.com*

**ISBN# 978-0-9636066-5-5**


**Printed in the United States of America**
**Copyright © 2007 by Frances A. Gillette**
**First Printing**

---

Additional copies of The Old Farmhouse Kitchen can be ordered for:  Hardcover...$27.95 plus $6.00 shipping = $33.95
Soft Cover...$19.95 plus $5.00 shipping = $24.95
**FRAN GILLETTE**
P.O. Box 351
Yacolt, WA 98675
360-686-3420
*Washington residents please add appropriate sales tax for your area.*


*Can be ordered from Gabrielle Massie online at www.simplyfocused.org*

What evokes the same happy memories as licking an ice cream cone, Mom's fresh cookies, the old swimming hole, gathering with your cousins and lots of the best food in the world? At least, in your own world! My goal with writing this Farm Cookbook is to provide the subtle ambiance of farm life as it was.........now created in your own kitchen! Whether you are a farm girl or a farmer, or just wish you were, this book will produce irresistible creations and charm. Within yourself, there must be the desire to cook a recipe with simple goodness, a recipe easy to follow that will, and does, provide refreshing success.

# AMERICAN FARMERS

# PULLING TOGETHER

## THIS BOOK IS DEDICATED TO ALL THE PAST, PRESENT AND FUTURE FARMERS OF AMERICA.

When I was a child, the following farmers were my heroes! They helped to feed my body and sustain my heart:

**My parents, Lucy and Chester Abernathy**
**My husband's parents, Francis and Rose Gillette**
**Uncle Paul and Aunt Margaret Abernathy**
**Uncle Claude and Aunt Elizabeth McDaniels**
**Pete and Ruth Kysar**
**Jake and Edel Kysar**
**Uncle Henry and Aunt Pearl Rotschy**
**Raymond and Ruth Heidegger**
**Uncle Ed and Aunt Lillie Rotschy**
**Bob and Bertha Kysar**

My heroes supplied so much for so many. They grew and harvested berries, giving jobs to us children and beautiful jam for winter time. They nurtured the chickens so they could produce good eggs and meat. They milked the bossy cows for the rich cream and milk. My heroes kept the work horses shod, fed, and working. They pastured healthy beef cattle and sheep. Lastly, these tireless providers hauled the pigs, cattle, sheep, and cans of cream to market. I will always remember them, remaining grateful for the work ethic and values that are their legacy.

# TABLE OF CONTENTS

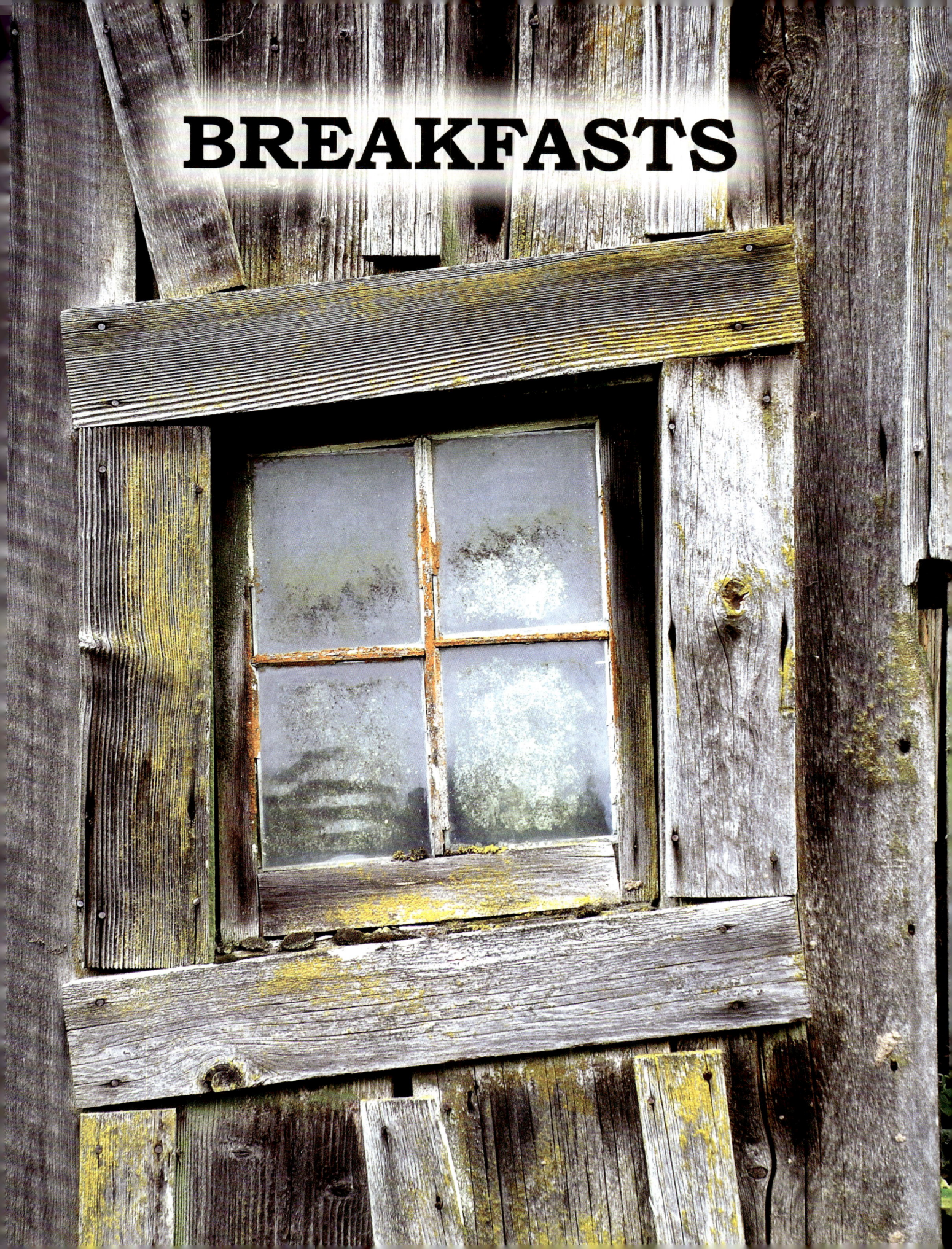

# BREAKFASTS

# DUTCH BABIES

This is a treat for my family on Sunday morn.

| PAN SIZE | BUTTER | EGGS | MILK & FLOUR |
|----------|--------|------|--------------|
| 2-3 quart | ¼ cup | 3 | ¾ cup each |
| 3-4 quart | ⅓ cup | 4 | 1 cup each |
| 4½ quart | ½ cup | 6 | 1½ cups each |

Select the recipe proportions to fit your pan. Put butter in pan and set into 425° oven. Mix batter quickly while butter melts. Put eggs in blender and whirl at high speed for 1 minute. With motor running, gradually pour in milk, then slowly add flour; continue whirling for 30 seconds. Remove pan from oven and pour batter into hot melted butter. Return to oven and bake until puffy and browned, 20-25 minutes. Serve with syrup or lemon juice.

# POTATO PANCAKES

From Karen Glafka with some changes by Fran.

**4 raw potatoes** (medium size)
**3 eggs**
**2 Tbsp. flour**
**½ small onion**
**¼ tsp. salt**
**Dash of pepper**

Grate potatoes and onion. Beat eggs, add rest of the ingredients and mix together; then fry like pancakes.

# AUNT PEARL'S PANCAKE

Aunt Pearl says, "How you cook the pancake is part of the secret of a good pancake!" Like her son-in-law Ward always said, "When there's lots of bubbles, turn it! And don't keep flipping the pancake."

**2 eggs**
**2 cups buttermilk**
**2 cups flour**
**2 tsp. baking soda**
**1 tsp. salt**
**2 tsp. sugar**
**¼ cup oil**

Mix all the ingredients together. If batter is too thick, use milk to thin it, or use sour or sweet cream for especially good flavor.

# HUCKLEBERRY SYRUP

**2 cups huckleberries**
**2 Tbsp. lemon juice**
**½ cup sugar**
**½ cup water**

Boil 1 cup huckleberries, lemon juice, sugar, and water. Simmer for 5-8 minutes. Remove from heat, add 1 cup huckleberries. Serve warm over pancakes and waffles.

# MAPLE SYRUP

From daughter-in-law, Tina. With eleven hungry farm children, much syrup is used! Fabulous flavor.

**½ cup butter**
**½ cup sugar**
**¾ cup brown sugar**
**¼ cup corn syrup**
**¾ cup heavy cream**
**½ tsp. maple flavoring**

Cook together, stirring constantly over medium heat, until slightly thickened, about 5 minutes. Keep warm and serve over pancakes and waffles.

It's the coffee that wakes up all the flavor of any pancake!

# FLUFFY BUTTERMILK PANCAKES

The egg whites and buttermilk make these pancakes light and fluffy.

**3 eggs, separated**
**1⅔ cups buttermilk**
**1½ cups sifted flour**
**1 tsp. baking powder**
**1 tsp. baking soda**
**1 tsp. salt**
**1 Tbsp. sugar**
**3 Tbsp. melted butter**

Beat egg whites and set aside. Beat yolks, add buttermilk, and dry ingredients, and stir just enough to mix. Blend in butter. Fold in egg whites. Fry on lightly-greased skillet over medium heat. When bubbly on top, flip.

# SWEDISH PANCAKES

Becky Abernathy's pancake recipe.

**3 eggs**
**1¼ cups milk**
**¾ cup flour**
**1 Tbsp. sugar**
**½ tsp. salt**

Beat eggs until thick and lemon colored. Stir in milk. Sift dry ingredients; add to egg mixture, mixing till smooth. Drop by tablespoons onto moderately hot griddle. Spread batter evenly to make thin pancakes.

# SATISFYING PANCAKES

A favorite pancake at our home. You feel life is real good when you are eating this healthy pancake!

**½ cup oatmeal**
**½ cup corn meal**
**2 cups buttermilk**
**1 egg**
**1 Tbsp. oil**
**1 cup flour**
**2 Tbsp. brown sugar**
**1 tsp. baking soda**
**½ tsp. salt**
**½ cup pecan pieces**

Combine oatmeal and corn meal in a mixing bowl; stir in buttermilk. Let sit for 10 minutes. Stir in eggs and oil. Add dry ingredients; stir until smooth. Add pecans. For thinner pancake, add ½ cup milk. Fry on lightly-greased skillet over medium heat; flip when bubbly. Serve with fresh strawberries or raspberries.

# YEAST BUTTERMILK PANCAKES

Recipe from the kitchens of Clara Halme and Elaine Johnston

1 quart buttermilk
2 Tbsp. baking soda
2 Tbsp. sugar
1 tsp. salt
6 eggs, well beaten

4 cups flour
2 Tbsp. baking powder
1 pkg. yeast
¼ cup oil
1 cup cream or milk

Mix first four ingredients. Add flour, yeast, oil, and baking powder. Fold in eggs. Refrigerate overnight. Take out in the morning to activate the yeast. Add milk or cream. Can be refrigerated for a week. Fry on lightly-greased skillet over medium heat; flip when bubbly.

Hello,

When you serve my pancakes,
Light and fluffy like a cloud,
How your folks'll praise you,
And oh! Will you be proud!
They'll say that, as you baked 'em,
So rich and golden brown,
Though I may be the Pancake Queen,
'Tis you should wear the crown!
                    Love,
                    Aunt Jemima
                    FARM JOURNAL
                    Circa 1940's

# APPLE BUTTER

So good on pancakes!

1 dozen apples
6 cups apple juice
2 cups sugar
2 tsp. cinnamon
½ tsp. allspice
Pinch of cloves

Wash and quarter apples, removing inside seeds, etc. Cook apples and juice until apples are soft. Mash and sieve mixture. Add sugar and spices; cook slowly, stirring often for about 45 min. to an hour. I sometimes cook this in the oven. Makes 3 pints.

# SHEEPHERDERS POTATOES

Everyone wants this recipe from Gloria Royce. This recipe must be made in a cast iron pan with lid.

1 lb. bacon, good quality
8-10 cups red potatoes, sliced
¼ tsp. pepper
1 large sweet onion, sliced

Layer bacon in the bottom of the cast iron pan. Pour the potatoes on top of bacon. Add pepper, next add sliced onions. Set stove top to med-low. Put on lid. DO NOT touch for 1 hour! Serve with eggs of choice.

If I take the wings of the morning, and dwell in the uttermost parts of the sea; Even there shall thy hand lead me, and thy right hand shall hold me.

~PSALM 139: 9,10

6

# COFFEE KUCHEN

From Mary Muonio. A grand recipe!

**2 cups scalded milk**
**½ tsp. salt**
**1 pkg. yeast dissolved in ¼ cup**
  **warm water**
**1 cup shortening**
**2 eggs**
**1 cup sugar**
**1 tsp. lemon extract**
**Flour to make soft dough**

**FILLING:**
**1 quart sweet or sour cream**
**1 cup sugar**
**6 beaten eggs**

Mix and boil until thick, stirring often.

**1 cup stewed fruit per pan**
**Cinnamon**
**Sugar**

Mix all ingredients and make soft dough.  Let rise, stir down.  After the second or third time, roll out and put in pie tins.  When it rises, prick with a fork.  Put stewed fruit on top (peaches, prunes, apricots, apples, etc.).  Pour cooled filling on top of fruit.  Sprinkle with cinnamon and sugar.  Bake at 350° for about 45 minutes.

# QUICK AND EASY BREAKFAST CASSEROLE

From Esther Jolma. Esther and I have shared many days together in the strawberry fields. Where have the years gone?

**4 slices of bread (any kind)**
**1 lb. bulk sausage or sausage links**
**1 cup grated sharp cheddar cheese**
**6 eggs**
**2 cups milk**
**1 tsp. salt**
**dash pepper**

Tear up bread and place in greased 9"x 13" baking dish. A pretty oven-to-table casserole would be a good choice. Brown sausage and drain well (if using links, slice). Add sausage. Sprinkle with cheese. Beat together eggs, milk, salt, and pepper. Pour over mixture in pan. Bake in preheated 350° oven for 35-40 minutes. The cheese will rise to the top during baking. Optional additions: onions, green olives, mushrooms, parmesan cheese, paprika. Can be prepared the night before; just cover, refrigerate, and bake in the morning.

# SOUTHERN-STYLE BREAKFAST

With our southern heritage our children were raised on hominy grits. Try this great recipe!

**1 lb. sausage**
**3½ cups water**
**1 tsp. salt**
**1 cup quick cooking grits**
**2 cups cheese, grated**
**4 large eggs, beaten**
**¾ cup milk**
**¼ cup butter**
**¼ tsp. pepper**

Brown and crumble sausage, drain. Set aside. Bring water to a boil; stir in grits. Reduce heat and simmer 5 minutes, stirring occasionally. Remove from heat; add 1 cup cheese, stirring until melted. Add sausage, eggs, and remaining 3 ingredients. Put grits in a casserole dish, sprinkle with 1 cup cheese. Bake at 350° for 30-40 minutes.

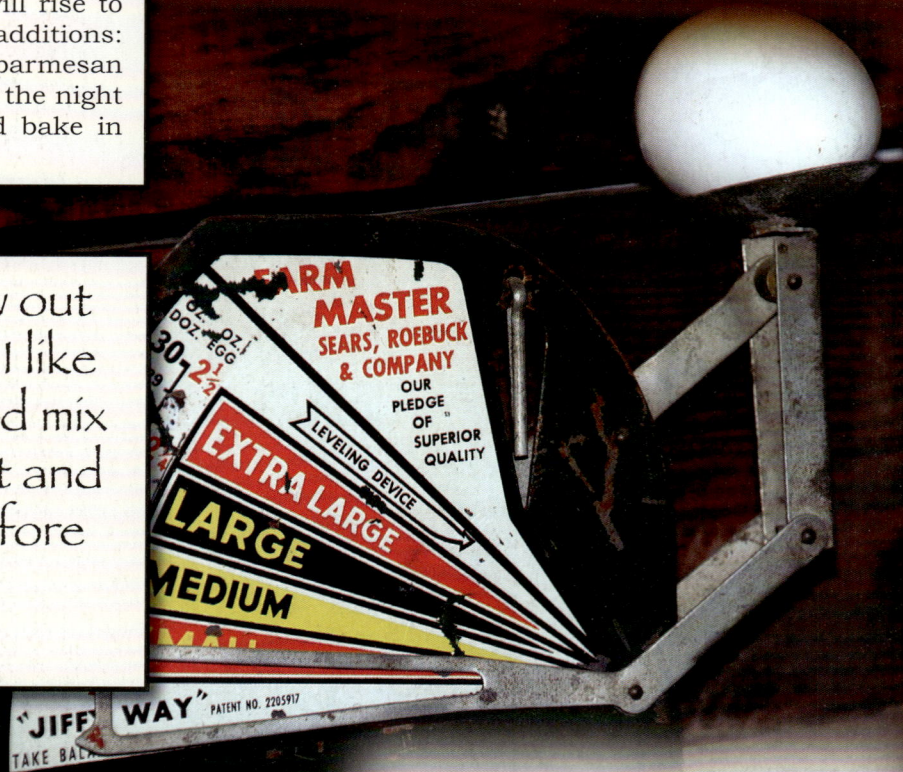

"Some people throw out their bacon grease. I like bacon grease. I would mix it with a little sawdust and start a fire with it before throwing it out"

-Pete Kysar, 89 ½ yrs.

FARM MASTER
SEARS, ROEBUCK & COMPANY
OUR PLEDGE OF SUPERIOR QUALITY
LEVELING DEVICE
EXTRA LARGE
LARGE
MEDIUM

"JIFFY WAY" PATENT NO. 2205917
TAKE BAC

My husband, Sonny, ordered this egg weigher when he was 9 years old, from the Sears Roebuck catalog. He had his own egg business.

# THE BEST SCONES

From Cheri Mattson. Cheri worked with a scone recipe until she made it to perfection. This is a soft, tender scone.

Sift together:

**2 cups flour**
**⅓ cup sugar**
**3 tsp. baking powder**
**¼ tsp. salt**

Cut into flour mixture like pie crust:

**½ cup butter**

Mix together in a cup:

**¾ cup sour cream**
**1 egg**
**1½ tsp. vanilla**

Add to dry ingredients until soft dough forms.

Roll into 8-inch disk. Cut into wedges. Separate. Bake at 375° for 12-15 minutes. Excellent if served hot. If adding chocolate chips, nuts, berries, or cranberries, mix in with flour before sour cream.

Cheri says, "You can substitute whipping cream or milk, if you desire, for the sour cream. I use sour cream exclusively."

# CRACKED WHEAT MUSH

We call this delicious breakfast food mush; you probably call it hot cereal.

**2 cups cracked wheat**
**1 cup chopped pecans or almonds**

Toast cracked wheat and nuts in a 400° oven until roasted, about 5 minutes. Cool. Place cereal in a tight container.

**For 4 servings, combine:**
**3 cups boiling water**
**1 tsp. salt**
**1 cup toasted wheat mixture**

Bring to boil and simmer until tender, about 40 minutes. Stir occasionally. To serve, use Half & Half with brown sugar. I like butter on mine. We also serve with dried cranberries, raisins, or dates.

# OLD FASHIONED BAKED OATMEAL

Well! I am an older woman and I had never made or tasted this delightful dish. We were staying a night with Liz and Stan Uskoski; she fixed this for breakfast with berries and cream. Rick and Dawn Massie were there also and Dawn informed me that this is a favorite in their family. You better try it, it is good!

**3 cups oatmeal, quick or old**
  **fashioned**
**1 cup brown sugar**
**2 tsp. baking powder**
**1 tsp. cinnamon**
**1 tsp. salt**
**1 cup milk**
**½ cup butter, melted**
**2 eggs, beaten**

In mixing bowl, combine ingredients. Spoon into a 9 inch square baking pan. Bake at 350° for 30-40 minutes. Serve warm with cream, milk, butter or whatever you like. Berries are excellent on top. When you double this recipe it fits in a 9"x 13" pan.

# BREADS

# WHITE BREAD

This recipe from Elaine McDaniels is superb. Elaine says, "The secret: knead well and let dough rise a long time."

MIX WELL:

**17 cups flour**
**2 Tbsp. salt**

DISSOLVE:

**7 cups water**
**½ cup sugar**
**2 scant Tbsp. yeast**
**⅛ cup butter**

Mix dry ingredients into yeast mixture. Add a bit more flour if dough is sticky. Knead well. Work butter into dough and knead. Let rise until double in bulk. Knead 8-10 minutes and let rise again; make into loaves. Let rise until double in bulk—possibly 2 hours. (Variations: flatten dough until ½-inch thick. Let rise 15 minutes. Prick with fork. Bake on cookie sheet. After 15 minutes, take bread off cookie sheet and bake until golden brown. Take out of oven and wrap in dish towel.) Bake bread loaves at 375° for 40 minutes. Brush tops with shortening.

# FAVORITE WHITE BREAD

I make this recipe often! Beautiful big loaves of fine-grained textured bread. The shortening kneaded into the dough makes the difference!

**6 cups warm water**
**3 Tbsp. yeast**
**¾ cup sugar**
**3 Tbsp. salt**
**½ cup shortening**
**Flour**

In large mixing bowl dissolve yeast with sugar in 6 cups of warm water. When yeast starts to work add salt and begin mixing in flour. Mix enough flour until dough starts to clean sides of bowl. Pour out on a floured surface and knead until it comes together. Knead in ½ cup shortening. Continue kneading until smooth. Place dough in a greased bowl, let rise until doubled. Punch down; shape into 5 loaves. Place each loaf into a greased pan. Let rise until doubled. Bake at 375° for 40-45 minutes.

## NO-YEAST BROWN BREAD

Selma Stephenson was well-known for her loaves of brown bread.

⅔ cup sugar
2 or 3 Tbsp. shortening or butter
½ cup molasses
3 cups whole wheat flour
1 tsp. baking powder
1½ tsp. salt
2½ cups buttermilk

Mix in order given. Raisins, nuts, or seeds can be added. This makes 2 small size loaves or 1 large loaf. Bake at 325° for 45 minutes to an hour.

## RAISIN-NUT WHOLE WHEAT BREAD

Everyone wants this recipe after tasting this good bread. Full of good rich old time flavors. I make round loaves.

4 cups water
3 Tbsp. yeast
½ cup molasses
½ cup brown sugar
2 Tbsp. salt
2 cups raisins
2 cups chunked walnuts
4 cups white flour
1 cup 10-grain cereal
Whole wheat flour

In large mixing bowl dissolve yeast in water and sugar. Blend in the rest of ingredients using whole wheat flour until dough goes away from bowl. Turn out dough to floured surface and knead for 8-10 minutes, let rise in greased bowl until doubled in size. Place in greased pan and let rise until double. Bake at 350° for 35-40 minutes.

"I can not put into words the sense of pride and honor that I feel for serving and fighting for this great nation."

-SERGEANT Remington, Brian  USMC
Served in Iraq
Drill Instructor MCRD San Diego

5TH YEAR SERVING AMERICA

As a child ... If you were lucky to have known an orderly, secure home, a place of love and comfort, you were lucky enough. For a happy home is a place to belong: to parents, to sisters and brothers, but most of all yourself. One of my earliest memories of belonging was on a cold front porch where I lived in Yacolt. I was 6 years old, one of a large family. The new sun was just touching the dew so the grass and trees were sparkly (like Mama's pretty dishes). The air was shivery, crystal clear, and puffed out of my mouth in little white clouds. It was a "blue bird day" (like my Daddy always said). That spring morning it was my turn to bring in the fresh milk and cream that the nice milkman, Dick Rinta, delivered for us before anyone was up. (The cows must of got up awfully early then.) He would set out real glass bottles with skinny necks and little paper hat lids on top. The bottles of milk weren't pure white but kind of foggy white and they were ours! If I hurried out of bed, I could watch him walk back to his square blue milk truck with the big brown Jersey cow's head painted on the side. Mr. Rinta wore a white cap and he sure knew how to whistle like the robins. Since it was my turn that morning to have the job, I savored the walk down our long hallway making the turn last. I was wearing my favorite nightgown, the cozy- to-my-toes-thick-one that could make an alligator-shaped head with my knees for eyes when I sat by the heater with my sisters. When I peeked out of the door and spied the fresh milk, my eyes would keep moving until I made sure the cream bottle was there too. The thick and rich "stuff" fostered a passion that is with me today. (Cream and butter are on my top 10 most favorite foods list!) As I carefully grabbed the bottle's neck and felt the cool wet glass, my mouth smiled big. Because in my little heart was the knowledge of Mama and Daddy's trust that I could lift and carry the good milk, the good cream, and not break the bottles. It was my first sense of the value of each person in a family. A sense of contributing, and without my turn maybe we wouldn't even get cream on our mush that morning. I would so gently carry them like a heavy gift, cradling the fullest part of the milk bottle tight to my tummy, and go back inside my warm home. I learned that the role of doing chores made me really an important part of my family. They belonged to me and I to them. We were a unit of measure—not unlike the gallons and half-gallons of Rinta's Jersey Dairy milk. It was a great place to be in 1968, in the best country on earth, in the best little town, in my own little self. –Heidi Esteb

14

# CAROLYN RINTA'S WONDERFUL BREAD

Carolyn Rinta says, "This recipe is my adaptation of a Washington State University Extension bulletin issued in 1949, when I was in a 4-H club. When Dick and I were dating, he wanted to know if I could bake bread, before our romance proceeded any further. He was relieved to learn I won the 4-H county bread contest!" Carolyn adds, "If you succeed with this recipe your husband will never leave you!"

**6 cups milk**
**6 Tbsp. oil or butter**
**½ cup honey**
**3 Tbsp. salt**
**2 envelopes yeast**
**1 cup lukewarm water**
**Approx. 16 cups flour (part whole wheat, part unbleached)**

Begin this right after breakfast while cleaning up the kitchen; pull the loaves out of the oven at supper time!

Into a large metal bowl, measure the milk (do not substitute powdered milk). Scald the milk, and then add the oil or butter (can omit if you use rich raw milk), the honey, and the salt. Set aside and let cool to lukewarm. While it is cooling, dissolve the yeast in the water. When the milk mixture is cool, add the yeast mixture and stir well. Then gradually add the flour, into the same bowl. Don't make the mass too stiff. Knead, knead, knead (for at least 10 minutes). Cover with a damp towel and let rise (don't put in to warm spot). After 3-4 hours, press down and turn over. Let rise again, push down, and shape into five loaves. Place in pans and let rise again. Bake at 375° for 40-45 minutes. Cool on wire racks.

**NOTE:**

Using milk as a liquid, not too much flour, less yeast, longer rising and shorter baking time are the keys to good, moist, fine-grained bread. This will not crumble when cut for toast or sandwiches. This can be used for cinnamon rolls, but is too moist and heavy to make good dinner rolls.

15

# CORN MEAL BREAD

Everyone likes this molasses bread. We've been making this recipe for years. Anadama bread: sooo country---sooo good!

**3 cups water**
**3 tsp. salt**
**⅔ cup yellow corn meal**
**⅔ cup light molasses**
**4 Tbsp. shortening**
**3 pkgs. yeast**
**1 cup water**
**2 Tbsp. sugar**
**6 cups flour, plus 4-5 cups flour**

Put cold water, salt, and corn meal on stove. The cold water with corn meal will prevent lumps. Boil and stir constantly for 2 minutes. Add molasses and shortening to hot mixture, stir well. Dissolve yeast in 1 cup water with sugar; add to cooled corn meal mixture. Mix well. Work in about 4-5 cups flour; dough should be easy to handle. Put dough on floured surface and knead for 8-10 minutes. Place dough in greased bowl and cover. Let rise until double in size. Punch down and cut into 3 pieces. Grease 3 round pans; sprinkle with corn meal. Put dough in pans and let rise until double. Bake at 375° for about 45 minutes.

Give us this day our daily Bread.

~Matthew 6

# RICH EGG BREAD

If you've never tackled breadmaking before, this is the recipe to try.

Measure into mixing bowl:

**¾ cup warm water**

Add and let dissolve:

**2 Tbsp. yeast
a little sugar**

After yeast mixture is dissolved, add and mix:

**1½ cups lukewarm milk
¼ cup sugar
1 Tbsp. salt
5 eggs
¼ cup soft butter
7 to 8 cups flour**

Mix with spoon until smooth. Add enough remaining flour to handle easily; mix with hands. Turn onto lightly floured board; knead 8-10 minutes; let rise; shape into 3 loaves. Bake until a rich brown at 375° for 30 minutes.

# MOLASSES BREAD

Grandma Tuominen's recipe. Given by Cheryl Crume. She says, "We always loved eating Grandma's homemade bread with real butter."

**10 cups flour – ½ white, ½ rye or
    whole wheat
3-4 pkg. yeast in 1 cup warm
    water
¼ cup melted shortening or oil
1 cup molasses
2½ tsp. salt
2 cups scalded milk**

Add shortening, molasses, salt, and milk into dissolved yeast. Stir in 3 cups flour and beat 2 minutes. Add remaining flour and knead for 10 minutes. Let rise 45 min. Punch down and divide into 3 equal portions. Shape into loaves, put in well greased pans. Let rise 40 min. Bake at 425° for 10 min, lower to 350° and bake for 25 min.

# FLUFFY WHOLE WHEAT ROLLS

From Bev Amundson, my favorite auctioneer!

2 Tbsp. dry yeast
¼ cup honey
½ cup warm water
1½ tsp. salt
1 cup warm water
½ cup butter
3 eggs
4-5 cups whole wheat flour

Dissolve yeast in ½ cup warm water. Cream butter and honey to a fine stream. Add eggs, one at a time, and beat. Add yeast mixture, add the 1 cup more of water, add flour and salt. Let rise until double. Knead, then let rest 3 minutes. For rolls—let rise and bake at 350° for 15-20 minutes. Very easy and sooo good!

"We Marines appreciate the gratitude from other Americans. It helps to hear the positive and belief in us. We are here every day because we choose to be. It's our job."

-LCPL Guiterrez, Adam USMC
Serving 3rd Tour in Iraq
July 30th, 2007

5TH YEAR SERVING AMERICA

Throughout my early years I was responsible for churning the butter! Butter for the table and for all the bakery. I'm remembering when oleo first was available. We all thought it was gold as we mixed the yellow color into the big bag full of white oleo. We would squeeze that bag with vengeance until all was golden. Now, I really wonder why my folks bought the stuff! On our farm we had an abundance of beautiful butter from our Jersey cow. We kept the butter in the old oak ice box or in the pantry. I guess the oleo was a novelty and it must have been cheap!

In this day and age few people have a butter churn. If you have a yen to make butter, I'll tell you an easy way to do so. Use heavy whipping cream. Pour cream into a quart jar. Shake the cream in the jar, making sure the lid is tight, until yellow crumbles of butter appear. Continue shaking until the butter becomes a lump. Pour out the liquid and put the butter into a bowl. Using a wooden spoon and very cold water, rinse the butter, using the spoon to work out the milky liquid until cold water is clear. Salt butter and savor "the beyond words taste."
You get an A+!
We usually used sour cream and then we had nice thick buttermilk. I do not know if sour cream from the store would be successful.

# REFRIGERATOR ROLLS

Aunt Margaret Abernathy gave my mother this recipe. Mother made these lovely buns all of my childhood years. Of course we used good homemade butter on everything in those days.

½ cup butter, melted & set aside
¾ cup milk, scalded
½ cup sugar
1 egg
1 tsp. salt
3 Tbsp. shortening
3½ cups flour
1 pkg. yeast

Add sugar, salt, and shortening to scalded milk, and cool to lukewarm. Dissolve yeast in 1 cup warm water (add 1 tsp. sugar). Add egg to yeast mixture; beat. Add yeast mixture to milk mixture; gradually add flour; knead. Let rise; knead again; let rise again. Can be refrigerated for several days. When ready for use, roll out dough to ½ inch thick. Cut with large cutter and dip totally in melted butter. Place on large ungreased cookie sheet; let rise again. Bake at 350° for 15-20 minutes or until golden brown.

# POTATO ROLLS

Aunt Lillie Rotschy was well known for her buns made with this recipe. She used real potatoes, not instant.

Put in mixing bowl:

**1½ cups warm water**
**2 Tbsp. yeast**
**⅔ cup sugar**

After this is dissolved, stir in:

**2 tsp. salt**
**⅔ cup shortening**
**2 or 3 beaten eggs**
**1 cup mashed potatoes**
   (Make the potatoes before starting
   and they'll be cooling)
**7 to 7½ cups flour** (Half whole
wheat flour makes excellent rolls)

Knead until smooth and elastic. Cover and allow to rise until double in bulk. Punch down, shape into dinner rolls or roll out and cut into buns. Place in greased pan; let rise until double. Bake at 350° for 20 minutes or until golden brown.

# HEATHER'S HEARTY BREAD

Heather made up this soft and tender bread recipe. Rave reviews when served.

**3 Tbsp. yeast**
**2 cups warm water**
**1 cup sugar**
**1½ cups buttermilk**
**½ cup butter, melted**
**2 eggs**
**6-8 cups flour**
**½ cup butter melted**
**Parmesan Cheese**

Mix together first 3 ingredients and let set while yeast dissolves. Add beaten eggs, buttermilk, melted butter, and salt. Stir in 6-8 cups flour until dough leaves the side of bowl or ball is formed. Place dough in greased bowl. Grease top of dough and cover with plastic wrap. Let rise until doubled. Form into 4 round loaves and put in greased round pans. Poke holes on top of dough. Pour ½ cup butter on the loaves. Sprinkle generously with parmesan cheese. Let rise for ½ hour. Bake at 350° for 30 minutes.

It was a challenge for me to get this recipe on paper. A handful of flour, 2 large pinches of salt, a large hunk of butter…here it is!!

## FRAN'S CINNAMON ROLLS

This dough is good with the caramel recipe on bottom of page. I usually frost the rolls.

**4 cups warm water**
**3 pkgs. yeast**
**6 Tbsp. sugar**
**6 Tbsp. butter**
**2 eggs**
**3 tsp. salt**
**1 cup mashed potatoes, optional**
**10 cups flour** (approximately)
**1 cup butter**
**4 cups brown sugar** (approximately)
**Cinnamon**

Frosting:

**¼ cup butter** (not margarine)
**1 (3oz.) pkg. cream cheese**
**1 lb. powdered sugar**
**Milk**
**1 tsp. vanilla**
**¼ tsp. maple flavoring**

Dissolve yeast and sugar in warm water. While yeast working, melt butter. Beat eggs in butter and add to yeast mixture. Add salt. Add potatoes here if desired. Add flour gradually until dough is stiff but soft. Turn out onto floured counter and knead about 1 minute. Place dough back in greased bowl and cover with plastic wrap. Let rise until double. Roll out on counter to ¼" thick. Spread with about ½ cup soft butter. Cover evenly with brown sugar using more or less to taste. Sprinkle on cinnamon. Roll up jellyroll fashion and cut in 1" to 1½" slices. Melt ½ cup butter; divide between 2 pans (9" x 13"). Place cut rolls in pans, cover and let rise until doubled. Bake at 350° for about 30 minutes. Frost either warm or cool.

**For change, replace the melted butter with the caramel recipe. Do not frost.**

Beat cream cheese and butter until smooth; add sugar and enough milk to make smooth frosting. Add vanilla and maple flavorings.

**Caramel for cinnamon rolls**
Combine in saucepan:

**1½ cups sugar**
**½ cup butter**
**½ cup light corn syrup**
**¼ cup water**

Bring to boil. Cook 3 minutes, stirring constantly. Pour into two greased 9" x 13" pans. Cool. May sprinkle with walnuts or pecans before adding dough pieces. Bake at 375° for about 20-25 minutes.

Nurture your mind with great thoughts; to believe in the heroic makes heroes.     -Benjamin Disraeli

# MAPLE BARS & DONUTS

I have made and given this recipe to many. The only way you can tell how good and easy it is to try it! You will make this over and over! Mary Heidegger gave me this recipe years ago! I've changed a few things. She called this recipe "Spudnuts."

**Mix like pie crust:**

**6 cups flour**
**1 tsp. salt**
**4 Tbsp. sugar**
**½ cup shortening**

**Add to flour mixture:**

**2 cups milk** (warmed)
**1 egg, beaten**
**⅓ cup mashed potatoes**

Dissolve 3 pkgs. yeast in ½ cup or more of lukewarm water; add to above mixture. Use just enough flour so dough holds together—do not knead. Place in greased container and let rise 1 hour. Roll and cut into maple bars and donut shapes. Let stand 15 minutes and fry in hot oil.

## FROSTING:

Melt ½ cup butter in saucepan; stir in 1 cup brown sugar and bring to boil, stirring over low heat for 2 minutes. Stir in ¼ cup milk; bring to boil, stirring constantly. Cool to lukewarm; gradually stir in 1¾ to 2 cups powdered sugar and a few drops of maple flavoring.

Show extra respect for people whose jobs put dirt under their fingernails.
AMERICAN FARMER

26

# DOUGHNUT BALLS

From Ardith Rosenlund. They're so easy to make and simply delectable! Good for breakfast or anytime.

1½ cups flour
2 tsp. baking powder
½ tsp. salt
⅛ tsp. nutmeg
½ tsp. cinnamon
½ cup sugar
½ cup milk
1 Tbsp. oil
1 unbeaten egg

Mix together and drop by teaspoons into hot oil. Fry until done. When warm, roll in sugar.

# THIS IS AMERICA

Our land has been a beacon for over 200 years to people everywhere. The stars and the stripes shine through it all: The good, the plenty, the hardships and toil. Our nation's light shines for us, illuminating the path to personal blessings and individuality. She is a safe harbor for the sails of freedom, allowing God's governing hand to guide and strengthen. We Americans have always been just as noted for our laughter as for our smile. And when you consider it, why shouldn't Americans smile? There's the American spring bringing new greens for the table. And the American summer, hot and generous in all her glorious harvest. And the American autumn, sweet and hardy as a Northern Spy apple. And after these, the American winter, white and watering all, waiting to bring new life again. And still in the background, is the huge, majestic, and unconquerable country. Most Americans know what they have; not many of them are afraid. They can afford to smile contemptuously at evil while helping to destroy it. In the gardens and fields, in the faces of men, in the kitchens across our land, this common feature of America is its smile. May your smiles grow in number as these recipes warm your hearts. May God Bless America.

On 2001, Sept. 11, our nation was attacked. For six long years our wonderful service men and women have been fighting overseas. They continue to sacrifice while protecting and defending our freedoms. We must remember to thank them and pray for their safe return.

# ORANGE BUTTER ROLLS

This is a special treat for everyone. I always make a double recipe and try to make them last until the next day.

Dissolve in large bowl:

**2 Tbsp. yeast**
**½ cup warm water**
**¼ cup sugar**

Mix in:

**1 tsp. salt**
**½ cup sour cream**
**2 eggs**
**⅓ cup melted butter**

Mix in:

**About 3 cups flour**

Filling:

**1 cup toasted coconut** (reserve ¼ cup)
**1 Tbsp. grated orange rind**
**Softened butter**

Orange glaze:

**¾ cup sugar**
**½ cup sour cream**
**2 Tbsp. orange juice concentrate**
**¼ cup butter**

Combine in saucepan and boil 3 minutes, stirring occasionally.

Gradually add flour to form stiff dough. Grease bowl and top of dough. Cover with plastic wrap. Let rise until doubled. Roll out half of dough to a circle about ¼ inch thick. Spread with butter and half of coconut-orange mixture. Cut into pie-like wedges and roll up from wide end. Place rolls point side down in a greased 9"x 13" pan. Repeat with remaining dough, adding cut rolls to same pan. Let rise for ½ hour. Bake at 350˚ for 30 minutes. Pour glaze over rolls and sprinkle with reserved coconut.

**The military quotes in this book are from service men and women who were raised with my grandchildren in the Yacolt – Battle Ground area. They are special!**

# PULLA YEAST BREAD

Ruth River's "Pulla" is unbeatable. She sells these delicious loaves to us at Christmas time.

1 cup warm water
4 Tbsp. yeast
1½ cups sugar
4 cups milk, warmed
1 Tbsp. salt
¾ cup butter, softened
6 eggs
1-2 Tbsp. crushed cardamom
    (depending on taste preference)
12 cups flour, approximately
**Nuts** (optional)

Add yeast and sugar to warm water. Add eggs, milk, salt, cardamom, and part of flour. Add butter and rest of flour. Mix well. Let rise, shape into braids. Let rise and brush with beaten egg. Add nuts and sprinkle sugar on top. Bake at 350° for about 20 min. Makes 8 loaves.

**Godliness with contentment is great gain.** -Apostle Paul

# THE OLD QUILT

It's a proud quilt with tears and rips!  This treasure was sent to my uncle in 1918 during World War 1 when he was stationed in England.  Three of my aunties stitched and embroidered this vintage cotton, silk, and taffeta cloth. Between them they sewed lines of crazy stitches, forming patterns.  My father found it in Uncle Lou's woodshed and now it is mine to love and cherish.

# ANGEL BISCUITS

So light and fluffy!

1 pkg. yeast
½ cup warm water
2½ cups flour
1 tsp. baking soda
1 tsp. salt

1 tsp. baking powder
⅛ cup sugar
½ cup shortening
1 cup buttermilk

Dissolve yeast in warm water; set aside. Mix dry ingredients in order; cut in shortening. Stir in buttermilk, and yeast and water. Blend in thoroughly and dough is ready to bake or it can be refrigerated. Turn out onto floured board and knead lightly as for regular biscuits. Let biscuits rise slightly. (If dough is too cold, it will take longer for them to rise than when first mixed.) Bake at 400° for 15-20 minutes.

## SWEET CREAM BISCUITS

An old recipe from Anna Abernathy's recipe file.

2 cups flour
4 tsp. baking powder which has
  been sifted with flour
1 tsp. salt
A little sugar if desired
1 cup sweet cream

Mix dry ingredients in a bowl. Add enough cream to make soft dough. Pat or roll out to ½ inch thick. Cut with biscuit cutter and place on greased pan. Bake at 400° for 10-12 minutes, or until golden brown.

## BUTTERMILK BISCUITS

Simple to make!

2 cups flour
4 tsp. baking powder
¼ tsp. baking soda
1 tsp. salt
½ cup shortening, chilled
1 cup buttermilk

Combine dry ingredients and cut in chilled shorten ing with a pastry blender until mixture is crumbly Add buttermilk, stirring just until dry ingredients ar moistened. Turn dough onto lightly floured surface Knead 4-5 times. Pat to ½ inch thickness. Cut Bake at 400° for 15-20 minutes.

Every clear day we see this beautiful view of Mt. St. Helens from our windows. We are most fortunate!

# ENGLISH MUFFINS

My niece Molly Kangas brought this great, easy recipe from South Dakota.

Scald:

**1 cup of milk**

Stir in:

**2 Tbsp. sugar**
**3 tsp. salt**
**½ cup butter**

Add:

**½ cup cool water**
**Dissolve 2 pkgs.**
**yeast in ½ cup**
**warm water**
**6 cups flour**

When milk mixture is lukewarm, blend in yeast mixture. Mix in flour a little at a time. Knead several times until dough is smooth and elastic. Let rise 1 hour or until double in bulk. Punch down; roll out on corn meal. Cut with 3 inch cutter. Let stand 30 minutes. Cook on griddle on top of stove (not oven). Turn when brown.

33

## EASY BLUEBERRY MUFFINS

These good muffins are popular at the Gillette Ranch.

2 cups frozen blueberries
2 eggs
2 cups milk
½ cup oil
4 cups flour
½ cup sugar
4 tsp. baking powder
2 tsp. salt

Mix all ingredients except berries. Do not over-mix. Grease muffin tins. Fold berries into mixture and immediately spoon into tins. Bake at 375° for about 25 minutes. Makes 18-20.

## POPOVERS

Hollow inside, crusty outside. Very marvelous with blackberry jam. You will want to double this recipe.

1 cup flour
½ tsp. salt
1 cup milk
2 eggs

Beat together until smooth. Do not over mix. Pour into well greased muffin pans about ½ full. Bake at 425° about 35-40 minutes. Serve hot out of the oven.

# BREAKFAST MUFFINS

A favorite at my house. Heidi carries on this tradition and serves these to company.

⅔ cup butter
1 cup sugar
2 eggs
3 cups flour
3 tsp. baking powder
1 tsp. salt
½ cup melted butter
1 cup sugar
1 tsp. cinnamon
1 cup milk

Mix together first 3 ingredients; add flour, baking powder, salt, and milk. Mix well. Spoon into greased muffin tins and bake at 350° for 20-25 minutes or until golden brown. Mix butter, sugar, and cinnamon; roll warm muffins into this mixture.

# CORN MEAL MUFFINS

A treat with soups, chili or by themselves.

2 cups corn meal
2 cups flour
2 Tbsp. baking powder
1 tsp. baking soda
¼ cup sugar
1½ tsp. salt
2 cups buttermilk
4 eggs, beaten
½ cup melted butter

Combine dry ingredients in a bowl. Beat together buttermilk, eggs, and melted butter; add to dry ingredients. Mix only until well moistened. Spoon into well greased muffin tins. Bake at 425° for 15-20 minutes.

# BERRY MUFFINS

Another good recipe from Becky Abernathy.

3 cups flour
½ cup sugar
1 Tbsp. baking powder
1 tsp. salt
½ cup brown sugar
½ cup melted butter
3 large eggs
1 cup milk
1½ cups berries

Sift dry ingredients into a bowl. Add brown sugar and stir to blend. Combine liquid ingredients and stir into dry mixture until just blended. Fold in berries very lightly and carefully. Spoon into well greased muffin tins. Bake at 400° for 20 minutes.

When you hear a robin's song, stop and think of dear Ole Hendrickson's words: "Listen to the birds singing early in the morning. They are praising and thanking God, their creator."

## DARK MOIST BRAN MUFFINS

Recipe from Jan Baysden.
You will make this recipe again and again.

**2 cups whole wheat flour**
**1½ cups pure bran**
**2 Tbsp. sugar**
**½ tsp. salt**
**1¼ tsp. baking soda**
**2 cups buttermilk**
**½ cup dark molasses**
**2 Tbsp. melted butter**
**Raisins if desired**

Combine dry ingredients; mix well. Combine remaining ingredients and add all at once to dry ingredients. Stir just enough to moisten. Fill greased muffin pans ⅔ full. Bake at 350° for 20-30 minutes. Makes 12-18.

## No Use In Going Along If You Don't Have To

"Them walking plows with two handles, if adjusted right, will need pulling but can go on their own. In 1935 me and Bob plowed 20 acres in Yacolt where the school is now. We more or less let the horses do it. I liked horses and they liked me. We each needed something from each other. I sat on one end of the field while Bob stayed on the other side. I'd get them going, set the plow up and say bye-bye. Bob would turn them around and send 'em back. As long as the horses could see us, they'd go all day. No use in going along if you don't have to."

-A TALE ABOUT TWO BROTHERS AS TOLD BY PETE KYSAR

# ZUCCHINI CARROT BREAD

This recipe comes from Char Lambert.
This bread stays moist for several days.
It freezes well. Delicious and nutritious!

3 eggs
1 cup oil
1½ cups brown sugar
1 cup grated zucchini
1 cup grated carrots
2 tsp. vanilla
2½ cups of whole wheat flour
½ cup all-bran cereal
1 tsp. salt
1 tsp. baking soda
3 tsp. cinnamon
1 cup chopped unblanched almonds

Preheat oven to 350°. Grease and flour 3 small bread pans. In large mixing bowl, beat eggs with oil. Stir in zucchini, sugar, carrots, and vanilla. Mix together flour, all-bran, salt, baking soda, and cinnamon. Stir in zucchini mixture. Add almonds and mix well. Bake for 1 to 1½ hours until toothpick inserted into center comes out dry. Allow to cool for 15 minutes in pan; then invert and cool on rack.

# BANANA BREAD

Make use of those ripe bananas! Lori brings us, and many others, this delicious bread. Spread slices with cream cheese when serving.

1¾ cups flour
2¼ tsp. baking powder
½ tsp. salt
⅓ cup shortening
¾ cup sugar
¾ tsp. grated lemon rind
   (optional)
2 eggs
1½ cups mashed
   bananas
½ cup chopped nuts

Mix together shortening, sugar, and lemon rind; blend until creamy. Beat in eggs and banana. Sift together flour, baking powder, salt, and add to sugar mixture. Beat well. Fold in nuts. Bake in one large or two small loaf pans for 50 minutes at 350°.

"Americans as a whole need to stop thinking of how bad we have it and realize how great it is to be a part of this nation".

-Corporal Gillette, Gregory USMC
Serving as Combat Engineer
August 23rd, 2007

4TH YEAR SERVING AMERICA

This old Pump House was built in the early 1950's over the well on Francis and Rose Gillette's farm in Yacolt, Washington. This quaint, charming little pump house still stands proudly and the livestock know there is water in the trough.

On the level, now, if everyone in the world was blind but YOU, would you need as many luxuries?

-H.L. Huntington

## KARLA'S PUMPKIN BREAD

Everyone wants this recipe! It is tried and true. From Karla Massie.

3 ⅓ **cups flour**
2 **tsp. baking soda**
1½ **tsp. salt**
1 **tsp. cinnamon**
1 **tsp. nutmeg**
3 **cups sugar**
1 **cup oil**
4 **eggs**
⅔ **cup water**
1 **can or 2 cups pumpkin**
1 **cup walnuts**
1 **cup raisins**

Combine all dry ingredients in a bowl. Add remaining ingredients and mix until smooth. Pour into greased and floured pans. Will make 3 medium loaves or 2 large loaves. Bake at 350° for 1 hour.

## CORN BREAD

A tender easy corn bread from Linda Walsten.

2 cups Bisquick
½ cup sugar
6 Tbsp. corn meal
½ tsp. baking soda
¾ cup butter
1 cup milk
2 eggs

Beat all ingredients and bake at 350° for 35 minutes in greased 9"x9" or double recipe and bake in a 9"x13".

## BUTTERMILK CORN BREAD

A southern treat. A crusty, yummy corn bread. When we were young, our mother made corn bread to eat with black-eyed peas. A warm, fuzzy memory!

3 Tbsp. melted butter
1 cup corn meal
1 Tbsp. flour
1½ tsp. baking powder
¼ tsp. baking soda
¼ tsp. salt
1 cup buttermilk
1 egg

Put melted butter in heated cast iron skillet or muffin tins. Combine corn meal and next 4 ingredients. Make a well in dry ingredients. Stir together egg and buttermilk, add to dry ingredients, stirring just until moistened. Pour into hot pans; bake at 450°.

## BLACK-EYED PEAS

Must try at least one time!

1 (16oz.) pkg. dried black-eyed peas
4 cups water
1 medium onion, chopped
½ tsp. pepper
1 tsp. salt
At least 1 lb. ham, cut into chunks
    or 1 ham hock

Boil and cook all together for approximately 1 hour or until peas are tender. Serve in bowls. Have plenty of corn bread, honey, and butter.

# SOUPS

"Serving my country has made me both a stronger person as well as a stronger woman. It has not been easy but it definitely has been worth it. It helps me knowing that I have the support from friends and family at home."

-Specialist Paoli, Traci US Army
Currently serving at Fort Bliss Texas.
September 10th, 2007
3RD YEAR SERVING AMERICA

44

# CHERI'S CREAMY POTATO SOUP

Daughter Cheri Mattson made up this creamy soup recipe.

1 small onion chopped fine
4 Tbsp. butter
6 potatoes
½ lb. of bacon, cooked/crumbled
1 can of Campbell's
   Cream of Potato soup, optional
⅓ cup of flour

3 cubes chicken bouillon
2 cups water
1 (8oz.) pkg. cream cheese,
   softened
4 cups milk

Saute onion in butter until tender. In large kettle, put water, bouillon, and potatoes with onion. Cover and cook until potatoes are tender. Blend cream cheese and flour until smooth. Stir into potato mixture. Add milk, bacon, and can of soup. Bring to boil and boil for 1 minute. Season with salt and pepper.
Very good soup base for clam chowder. Just omit can of soup; add 1 can clams, juice and all.

OVER THE RIVER AND THROUGH

# STEW WITH A ZING

From Linda Kysar.

2 cans pinto beans
1 can corn
2 lbs. hamburger
1 can chopped tomatoes
1 medium onion, chopped
1 Tbsp. dried onion powder
1 pkg. taco seasoning
1 pkg. Hidden Valley Ranch
    original dressing

Mix can of beans, corn, and tomatoes together into crock pot.  Do not drain.  In fry
pan, brown hamburger, onions, powdered
onion, and seasonings.  When browned, add
to crock pot and simmer on low.  Go to work
and come home to enjoy! Serve plain, with
sour cream and/or  grated cheddar cheese.

# MINESTRONE SOUP

Another winner from Char Lambert.

4 quarts beef stock
2 Tbsp. parsley
2 Tbsp. salt
1 tsp. pepper
1 tsp. oregano
3 large carrots, cut up
2 cups onion, chopped
5 stalks celery, cut up
1 pkg. frozen, chopped spinach
½ head cabbage, sliced
1 (16-oz.) can whole tomatoes
1 (16-oz.) can tomato paste
1 (16-oz.) can garbanzo beans
            with juice
Small can pork and beans
1 can kidney beans, drained
1 cup salad macaroni

Bring all ingredients to rolling boil.  Add 1
cup salad macaroni.  Top with parmesan
cheese when soup is done.

# HAM AND BEAN SOUP

Wonderful for the leftover ham bone.

1 1-lb. bag navy beans
1 medium onion, chopped
1 tsp. salt
Ham on bone or ham hocks
1 can evaporated milk
1 pint of Half & Half
1 (14oz.) can of chicken broth

Soak beans in hot water for 2 hours. Drain and put in large kettle. Add enough water to cover beans. Add ham bone. Cook slowly for about 1 hour; beans should be tender. Remove ham from bone; discard bone, skin, and fat. Add milk, Half & Half and broth.

# LENTIL SOUP

Lisa Rich says, "This is our family's favorite winter soup."

1 1-lb. bag of lentils
½ lb. bacon, diced
2 medium carrots, sliced
2 medium onions, sliced
2 quarts water
2½ tsp. salt
¼ tsp. pepper
¼ tsp. thyme
2 bay leaves
1 large potato, grated
2 ham hocks, or 1 large ham bone

Wash lentils 3 or 4 times; soak overnight in cold water. Saute bacon, onions and carrots until onion is transparent. Drain off ½ the bacon fat. In large kettle, add bacon to drained lentils; add water, salt, pepper, thyme, bay leaves, potato, and ham hocks. Simmer, covered, for 3 hours; stir occasionally. When lentils are tender, remove ham hocks, dice the meat from them and return to pan. Remove bay leaves.

# VEGETABLE SOUP

Very easy!

2 cups cooked chicken
2 quarts water or chicken broth
5 carrots, chopped
1 cup celery, chopped
¾ cup onion, chopped
1 cup dried noodles

Cook together until vegetables are tender. Add 1 cup dry noodles and boil another 10 minutes. Any veggie of choice may be added to this soup. Add more liquid as needed. We usually use leftover chicken from the day before.

# SALADS

# THE OLD BEAVER POND

Water lapped lazily against the log sprawled across the old beaver dam. Oh the fun of running, fishing and standing on that old log… Children dreaming dreams, dangling feet, and watching salamanders dart by made for a cherished afternoon. Being still and listening for the slap of a beaver's tail; and basking in the songs of the birds that sing in the heart of a child. Ahh, truly in tune with nature, wishing the day would never end.

~Linda Kysar

# NANCY'S SALAD

From Bev Amundson. Easy, but good. Bev took this recipe from her Aunt Nancy's recipe box.

1 head lettuce, cut up
½ bag Dorito chips, broken up

Cook in frying pan until browned;

1½ lbs. hamburger
½ onion, chopped

Add to frying pan mixture;

1 can red kidney beans, drained
1 can cheddar cheese soup
½ cup water
2 Tbsp. hot sauce

Pour mixture in frying pan over lettuce and chips. Stir well and serve HOT!

# YUMMY TACO SALAD

From my grand-daughter, Brooke Tormanen.

2 heads lettuce, cut up
½ bag plain tortilla chips, broken up
1½ lbs. hamburger
1 large can sliced olives, drained
1 bag Mexican shredded cheese
2 cups mayonnaise
2 pkgs. medium or hot taco seasoning
2 Tbsp. ketchup
2 Tbsp. milk
3 Tbsp. Pace Picante sauce

Brown hamburger in frying pan; drain well. Add 1 pkg. of taco seasoning to hamburger; cook, then let cool. Combine cooled meat, lettuce, olives, chips, and cheese in bowl; set aside. In small bowl combine mayonnaise, ketchup, milk and ½ to 1 whole pkg. remaining taco seasoning packet (depending on your taste) and stir to create a dressing. Add enough picante sauce to dressing to taste. Add dressing to salad, mix well.

# BROCCOLI-CAULIFLOWER SALAD

This comes from Krista Kaski, who says this is a family favorite.

1 head cauliflower
1 bunch broccoli
1 can black olives, sliced
1 cup mayonnaise
1 cup sour cream
1 pkg. Hidden Valley ranch dressing

Cut up cauliflower, broccoli and olives. Mix together mayonnaise, sour cream, and ranch dressing. Add to veggies and mix.

# CABBAGE PATCH SALAD

I'm sure you will "adopt" this salad recipe from Marilyn Mattson.

1 small head cabbage, shredded
2 Tbsp. sesame seeds
2 Tbsp. almonds, sliced
Salt and Pepper

**DRESSING:**
½ cup oil
2 Tbsp. sugar
1 seasoning packet from Top
   Ramen mix
1-2 pkg. Top Ramen noodles

Combine all salad ingredients and add whatever you have or like (broccoli, cauliflower, mushrooms, green onions, etc.).

Combine oil, sugar, and seasoning. Pour over salad and top with desired amount of crunchy Ramen Noodles.

Try different flavors of Top Ramen. You may also add chicken, shrimp or any other desired meat.

# ZESTY PASTA SALAD

This fresh, tasty, and EASY salad is from my daughter, Lori Homola.

**1 (16oz.) pkg. bow tie pasta**
**1 can olives, whole or sliced**
**2 cups grape tomatoes**
**2 cups yellow, red or orange bell peppers, sliced into thin strips**
**1 cup pepperoncini peppers, chopped**
**2 cups marinated artichoke hearts**
**Salt and Pepper to taste**
**1 cup zesty Italian dressing** (more or less to taste)

Boil pasta, drain, and rinse to cool. Cut and prepare all other ingredients into large bowl. Add pasta and dressing into bowl and mix well.

Other ingredients of your choice may be added.
Some good ideas are:
Fresh zucchini
Raw broccoli or cauliflower
Carrots
Cucumbers
Fresh mushrooms
Cheddar or feta cheese chunks
Chicken

Chilling pasta salads with Italian dressing for 1 hour before serving is recommended; more dressing may be added right before serving.

# PRETZEL SALAD

This yummy dish comes from Krista Kaski.

**3 Tbsp. sugar**
**2 cups crushed pretzels**
**¾ cup melted butter**

Mix and bake in 9"x13" pan at 350° for 15 minutes.

**1 cup powdered sugar**
**1 (8oz.) pkg. cream cheese** (softened)
**1 (8oz.) carton Cool Whip**
**2 cups miniature marshmallows**

Spread over crust and chill.

**2 (3oz.) pkg. strawberry JELL-O**
**2½ cups boiling water**
**2 (10oz.) pkg. frozen strawberries**

Mix together the boiling water and JELL-O. Stir to dissolve. Add the frozen strawberries. This will thicken as the strawberries melt. Pour over cream cheese mixture. Chill until set.

# SALAD WITH FRUIT AND PECANS

From Dottie Halberg. This salad is a phenomenal favorite!

**Bag of mixed herb spring mix**
**Bunch of red leaf lettuce**
**A few very thin slices red onion**
**1-2 pears, cut up**
**2 cups fresh strawberries, sliced**
**1 cup Craisins**
**½ cup Havarti cheese, grated**
**2 cups roasted pecans**

Coat pecans with corn syrup or honey; roast in 250° oven for ½ hour. Cool and add to lettuce mixture just before serving.

**DRESSING:**
**⅔ cup oil**
**½ cup sugar**
**⅓ cup lemon juice**
**1 tsp. Dijon mustard**
**½ tsp. salt**
**1 tsp. poppy seeds**

Mix together and pour over salad just before serving. Toss lightly.

You can make a similar lettuce salad with fresh pineapple or just pears. Always add roasted nuts and use the dressing below.

**DRESSING:**
**½ cup mayonnaise**
**1 cup Half & Half**
**Salt and Pepper**
**Poppy seeds, optional**

# MANDARIN DUET SALAD

We have made this wonderful salad of Paula Stephenson's for years.

**ORANGE GELATIN RING**
**2 pkgs. Orange JELL-O**
**2 cups boiling water**
**1 pint orange sherbet**
**1 can (11oz.) mandarin oranges,**
**drained**

Dissolve gelatin into boiling liquid; immediately add orange sherbet and stir until melted. Add oranges. Pour into 1½ quart ring mold. Chill until firm. Unmold and fill center with Ambrosia fruit salad.

# AMBROSIA FRUIT SALAD
**1 can (11oz.) mandarin oranges,**
**drained**
**1 can (13oz.) chunked pineapple, drained**
**1 cup flaked coconut**
**1 cup sour cream or 1 cup whipped**
**cream**
**1 cup cut-up marshmallows**

Mix all ingredients. Chill several hours or overnight.

## BROCCOLI DELIGHT SALAD

A favorite salad from Helen Hendrickson.

1 large bunch fresh broccoli, washed,
   drained, and cut in pieces (4-5 cups)
1 cup raisins
¼ cup diced red onion
10 strips bacon, fried and crumbled
1 cup sunflower seeds
3-4 Tbsp. sugar
½ cup light mayonnaise or creamy
   salad dressing
1 Tbsp. cider vinegar

Mix broccoli, raisins, onion, bacon, and sunflower seeds in glass bowl. Mix sugar, mayonnaise, and vinegar together and pour over salad.

## PASTA SALAD

This awesome salad is from Lynn Homola's kitchen.

4 cups macaroni noodles,
   cooked and drained
6 cups cooked, cubed
   chicken
1½ cups diced celery
4 cups grapes sliced in half
¼ cup mayonnaise
1 tsp. salt
1 tsp. poultry seasoning
½ tsp. onion salt
Dash of pepper
Cashews

Mix all ingredients together; add cashews before serving.

## BEAN SALAD

From Aunt Pearl Rotschy.

**1 can garbanzo beans, drained**
**1 can green beans, drained**
**1 can yellow wax beans, drained**
**1 can kidney beans, rinsed, and drained**
**1 can small green lima beans, drained**
**¼ cup thinly sliced onion**

Put beans and onion into bowl. Mix together the following and pour over beans:

**1 cup sugar**
**2 tsp. salt**
**½ tsp. pepper**
**½ cup oil**
**¾ cup cider vinegar**

Stir the salad several times over a 24 hour period and serve chilled.

## CUCUMBER TOMATO SALAD

A favorite at our house. Sonny brings in an abundance of summer vegetables from his garden. This is quick and easy—you can make as much as you want.

**Fresh tomatoes, peeled**
**Cucumber, peeled and cut into chunks**
**Sour cream**
**Mayonnaise**

Mix together equal amounts of sour cream and mayonnaise for the dressing. Pour over bowl of tomatoes and cucumbers. Salt and pepper to taste. There won't be any left!

# CUCUMBER DELIGHT

Our mother made these wonderful cucumber slices every summertime.

**Cucumbers, thinly sliced**
**Onion, thinly sliced**
**Cider vinegar**
**Water**
**Salt**
**Pepper**

Fill bowl ¾ full of cucumber and onion slices. Cover with water and add lots of salt and pepper. Let stand covered for 2 or more hours. Drain off water. Cover again with 1 part cider vinegar to two parts of water. Add more salt and pepper if desired. Mix well and serve.

# LAYERED LETTUCE SALAD

When I first tasted this salad, I knew that it had to be the best salad ever! My cousin, Lark Hersey, gave this recipe to me.

**head lettuce, cut up**
**cup celery, diced**
**eggs, hard boiled and sliced**
**cup frozen peas, cooked 1 minute and cooled; drain well**
**½ cup green pepper, sliced or diced**
**sweet onion, cut into rings**
**slices of bacon, fried and crumbled**

Layer all these ingredients in order listed into glass baking dish or bowl.

Mix together and spread over the top of salad like frosting:

**cups mayonnaise**
**Tbsp. sugar** (optional)
**Whatever salad seasoning you like**
**cup grated cheddar cheese**

Put grated cheddar cheese on top and refrigerate 8-12 hours.

59

# PERFECT HARD BOILED EGGS

I finally learned how to boil an egg after countless years and a million eggs!

Place eggs in single layer in a saucepan. Add water to a depth of 3 inches, and bring to rolling boil. When the water boils, cover pan with lid, and remove from heat. Let eggs stand for 14 minutes. Drain and return eggs to pan. Fill pan with cold water and ice, and let eggs stand for a few minutes to cool. Then crack shells on all sides on your countertop or other work surface. Peel under cold running water, starting at the large end.

There's more than one way to cook an egg, but we think this is the fastest for achieving perfect yolks. The secret is not to keep the water at a rolling boil the whole time.

# THE FARM HANDS' DEVILED EGGS

Everyone enjoys deviled eggs!

Cut in half a dozen hard-boiled eggs, peeled of shell and rinsed. Take out yolks and mash with fork. Set whites aside. Mix yolks with below ingredients:

**½ tsp. salt**
**¼ tsp. pepper**
**½ tsp. mustard**
**About ¼ cup mayonnaise**

You can use less mayonnaise and substitute vinegar, cream, or sweet pickle juice. Refill heaping amounts of egg yolk mixture into egg whites. Sprinkle with paprika.

# MAIN DISHES AND VEGETABLES

# WHOLE WHEAT NOODLES

2 cups whole wheat flour
1 cup white flour
1 tsp. salt
2 eggs
2 egg yolks
5 to 6 Tbsp. water
4 tsp. oil

Combine flour and salt in mixing bowl. Make a well in the middle and add eggs and yolks, 3 Tbsp. water and oil. Follow directions below adding more water as needed to make stiff dough. Divide into 3 parts and roll each part 12" x 24". Roll very thin. Slice into ¼" to ½" strips; dry 30 minutes before cooking. Cook uncovered 10 to 15 minutes.

# BEEF STROGANOFF

A luscious meal. With homemade noodles it is sure to be a hit!

2 lbs. round steak
¼ cup flour
½ cup butter
1 tsp. salt
¼ tsp. pepper
½ cup water
1 can cream of mushroom
    soup
¾ cup sour cream
½ cup milk

Cut steak into 2" x ½" strips. Coat steak with flour, salt, and pepper. Brown steak in butter. Cover and simmer about an hour. Stir occasionally. Stir in soup and continue simmering for a few minutes. Stir in sour cream and milk, heat thoroughly. Serve over noodles.

# CHICKEN AND NOODLES
Vera Dibert gave me this recipe.

**1 3-lb. chicken, cut up**
**Water**
**3 chicken bouillon cubes**

Place chicken in large kettle and cover with water. Add bouillon cubes and bring to a boil; reduce heat and simmer until thoroughly cooked, skimming top of water occasionally. Remove chicken pieces from broth and cool. Remove chicken meat from bone and add broth.

**NOODLES:**
**Flour**
**3 egg yolks**
**Water**
**Salt**

Put enough flour in a medium-sized mixing bowl so that when you make a 3-inch diameter "well" in flour there is still at least one inch of flour at the bottom of bowl. Beat together 3 egg yolks and ½ egg shell of water. Pour eggs and water in hole of flour; add a little salt. Use clean fingers to gradually stir flour into liquid. When it gets too thick to stir, work in as much flour as possible with hand. Work into piecrust shape on a floured board. Roll with rolling pin, as thin as possible, adding more flour to board as necessary. Dry noodles on flat surface. When dry, brush off excess flour. Roll up; cut roll in two pieces. Place one on top of other, and cut them to desired thickness. Separate noodles and dry over a chair covered with a clean cloth.

Bring broth to good boil; add noodles gradually. Cook slowly, about 30 minutes or until noodles are tender, stirring occasionally.

# SWEET AND SOUR CHICKEN WINGS

Unbeatable! Make these tasty wings and get raving compliments.
This recipe is in both of our other books.  Very, very good.

16-20 large chicken wings
2 eggs, beaten
½ cup milk
1 cup cornstarch
2 cups flour

**Sauce:**    Combine and bring to a boil 1½ cups brown sugar, 1 cup cider vinegar, ½ cup ketchup, ½ cup chicken bouillon, and 2 tablespoons soy sauce.

Salt and pepper chicken.  Add milk to beaten eggs.  Mix flour and cornstarch together.  Dip chicken wings into egg mixture and then into flour mixture.  Brown wings in hot shortening or oil in frying pan over medium-high heat.  Remove wings as they brown and place them in a 9"x 13" pan.  Pour sauce over chicken and bake at 350° for 35-45 minutes or until chicken is golden brown.

---

I do the very best I know how—the very best I can; and I mean to keep doing so until the end.  If the end brings me out all right, what is said against me won't amount to anything.  If the end brings me out wrong, ten angels swearing I was right would make no difference.

Abraham Lincoln (1809-1865)

---

# ASPARAGUS WITH BUTTERED PECANS

2 lbs. asparagus
6-8 Tbsp. butter
½ cup pecans, chopped
2 Tbsp. lemon juice
½ tsp. salt
¼ tsp. pepper

Cook asparagus in boiling water for 8 minutes, drain.  Melt butter in small saucepan.  Add pecans.  Cook and stir until butter and nuts are golden brown. Add lemon juice, salt, and pepper.  Spoon over warm asparagus.

## BREADED RANCH CHICKEN

From Faye Uskoski.

¾ cup corn flakes
¾ cup grated parmesan cheese
1 envelope ranch dressing
8 boneless chicken breasts
   (or about 25 chicken tenders)
½ cup butter

Rub melted butter on chicken pieces and roll in first three ingredients that have been mixed together. Bake in uncovered greased pan 45 minutes for breasts and about 25 minutes for tenders at 350°.

## CAULIFLOWER WITH CHEESE SAUCE

Always a hit!

1 large head cauliflower or 2
   medium heads
½ cup butter
¼ cup flour
3 cups milk
2 cups grated cheddar cheese
½ tsp. salt
¼ tsp. pepper

Cook cauliflower whole or break into pieces. Do not cook too long, only until fork-tender. Melt butter in pan, stir in flour and cook until mixture bubbles. Add milk. Cook and stir until boiling and thickened. Remove from heat; add cheese, salt, and pepper. Stir until cheese melts. Spoon cheese sauce over cauliflower. Serve.

# CHICKEN AND DUMPLINGS

An old fashioned, stick-to-the-ribs, satisfying meal.

**1 chicken, cut up**
**Salt, Pepper, Seasoning**

Cook chicken pieces until done in 2 quarts of water, with salt, pepper, or other seasonings.

Stir together:
**1½ cups flour**
**2 tsp. baking powder**
**¾ tsp. salt**

Cut in:
**3 Tbsp. shortening**
**Stir in ¾ cup milk, only until blended**

Drop by spoonfuls into chicken. Cook slowly for 10 minutes with pan uncovered. Then cook for 10 more minutes with lid on pan. Sometimes I add at least 1 cup of Bisquick to the above recipe and a little more milk. Very fluffy dumplings.

# ROAST CHICKEN AND VEGETABLES

We've been making this good chicken meal for years; everyone loves it. We make a cream gravy to put on the spuds.

**1 large whole chicken, washed,**
**    with fat removed**
**8 medium potatoes, chunked**
**12 carrots, peeled and chunked**
**Salt and Pepper**

**1 cup brown sugar**
**½ cup catsup**
**2 tsp. cider vinegar**

Salt and pepper chicken; place in roaster with breast up. Roast at 350° for 1 hour. There will be juices in bottom of roaster. Add potatoes and carrots, salt, and pepper. Roast for another hour. Mix brown sugar, catsup, and vinegar together and pour over chicken 20 minutes before done.

# HEARTY ROAST BEEF HASH

Our children were raised on hash. We served hash for the evening meal from left-over roast beef or venison.

Easy recipe, but you must have a grinder to make this nourishing and tasty hash.

**4 cups roast beef, cut up**
**6 cups raw potatoes, cut up**
**1 medium onion**
**Salt and Pepper to taste**

Grind these ingredients together, put in a bowl and mix well. Add about a cup of yesterday's brown gravy or Half & Half. Make into patties. Fry, turning when brown, until done.

# HOME-STYLE POT ROAST

There is nothing better than a tender piece of roast beef after a long day.

**3½-4 lb. chuck roast** (it can be frozen,
just allow more time for roasting)
**Salt and Pepper**
**Garlic salt**
**3-4 medium carrots** (cut into chunks)
**1 medium onion** (cut into chunks)
**4-5 medium potatoes** (cut into chunks)

Salt and pepper all sides. I always sprinkle lavishly with garlic salt.
Place in roaster with water about 1" high in roaster. Bake the roast on
325° for several hours (2½-3½). Then add carrot, onion, and potato
pieces. Roast about 45 minutes. May need to add more water.

# BAKED HAM

We always buy a ham with a bone in it, sometimes cooked and sometimes uncooked. Cooking the already cooked ham will improve flavor and texture. A scored ham with cloves in each scored square is attractive and tasty. A glaze is also good.

For already cooked, bone-in ham (10 lb.), roast for 1½ hours at 350°. This will slice nicely when ham sets for 20 minutes out of oven. Read directions on ham if uncooked, for time.

# SCALLOPED POTATOES AND HAM

My sister Linda always brings these flavorful potatoes to our Christmas gatherings. However, she triples this recipe.

**3 Tbsp. butter**
**3 Tbsp. flour**
**½ tsp. salt**
**¼ tsp. pepper**
**2½ cups milk**
**6-7 potatoes, sliced thinly**
**¼ cup onion, chopped finely**
**2 cups ham, cut in pieces**
**Butter**

Make a white sauce out of the first 5 ingredients, stirring constantly until smooth and bubbly. Layer ⅓ of the potatoes, ½ of onion and ham, and ⅓ of the white sauce in a casserole; repeat. Top with remaining potatoes and white sauce. Dot with 1-2 Tbsp. butter. Cover and bake 30 minutes. Uncover and bake about 1 hour or until potatoes are soft. Linda uses part ham juice in place of milk.

# CHERRY CARAMEL SAUCE

Everyone rants and raves about this good sauce over sliced ham.

**1 cup brown sugar**
**½ cup light Karo syrup**
**1 cup water**
**1 can cherry pie filling**

Mix and boil together for about 5 minutes. Add pie filling, mixing well. Pour over sliced ham.

# SLOP BREAKFAST

This recipe is from my sister-in-law, Corinne Abernathy, who got the recipe from her niece, Tammy Sarkinen.

**1 lb. Jimmy Dean sausage**
Brown in skillet and divide in half.

**6 potatoes, cut up**
**1 medium onion, chopped**
Fry in skillet with sausage grease.

**2 cups white sauce or gravy**
**12 eggs, scrambled**

Mix eggs with ½ of sausage, potatoes, and onion. Make white sauce or gravy of choice and add rest of sausage. Pour white sauce and sausage over eggs and potato mixture. Freshly diced tomatoes can be added on top.

Never eat more than you can lift.
-MISS PIGGY

# FRIED CHICKEN

There are many ways to fry chicken. This recipe is great! Sometimes just plain flour, salt, and pepper satisfies the palate. Grandma Lucy always fried chicken southern style using flour, salt, pepper and ½ inch of shortening for frying. Fry uncovered until crisp and done. Southern fried chicken is so good on a picnic or for lunch in the huckleberry fields.

**1 fryer chicken cut in pieces**
   (approx. 3 lb.)
**1 cup buttermilk**
**Shortening**
**1 cup flour**
**1½ tsp. salt**
**1 tsp. pepper**

Place chicken in large flat dish. Pour buttermilk over chicken. Refrigerate at least an hour. Combine flour, salt and pepper. Drain chicken pieces. Toss in flour mixture, one piece at a time. Shake off excess and dry on waxed paper for 15-20 minutes. Melt shortening ½ inch deep in large skillet. Brown chicken on all sides. Cover and simmer, turning occasionally for about 45 minutes. Uncover and cook 10 more minutes.

# COUNTRY GRAVY

For any milk gravy, use pepper generously, as it enhances the flavors. I will never make country gravy without thinking of my father. Grandpa Chester loved milk gravy for breakfast on pancakes, for lunch on biscuits or for supper on spuds.

**Leave ¼ - ½ cup drippings in skillet. Over medium heat, stir in 3-4 Tbsp. flour until bubbly. Add 3 cups milk or 1½ cups milk and 1½ cups water. Cook and stir until thick and boiling. Add more water if too thick. Season with salt and pepper. Serve with chicken and mashed potatoes and/or buttermilk biscuits.**

## The stomach is the kitchen of the soul.
### – Martin Luther

# POTATO SALAD

Everyone makes potato salad a little different. I usually throw in "a little of this and a little of that." Green onions, mustard, celery, celery seed, or dill pickles can be added.

**8 to 10 medium cooked red potatoes or**
   **yellow Yukon potatoes, cubed,**
   **cooked with 1 onion, chopped**
**1 dozen boiled eggs, chopped**
**1½ cups mayonnaise**
**½ cup sour cream**
**3 Tbsp. sugar**
**3 Tbsp. cider vinegar**
**Salt and Pepper to taste**

Mix all together and toss to coat. Cover and refrigerate.

# OVEN STEW

You are in for a treat.
From Paula Stephenson.

**3 lb. round steak** (cut in 1 inch pieces)
**2 cups potatoes** (cut in big chunks)
**2 cups carrots, big pieces**
**1 cup celery** (cut into chunks)
**1 cup onion** (cut into chunks)
**1 can tomato soup**
**2 cans water**
**1 Tbsp. sugar**
**3 Tbsp. flour**
**Salt and Pepper to taste**

Before adding soup mixture assemble meat and vegetables in order in a covered casserole. We use a cast iron dutch oven. Combine soup, water, sugar, and flour. Whisk until smooth. Pour soup mixture over layered vegetables. Cook 225° for 5 hours.

# MEAT LOAF

Warm from the oven, it is delicious accompanied by mashed or baked potatoes; good cold in sandwiches

**1½ pounds of hamburger**
**½ pound pork sausage**
**1 egg**
**¾ cup quick oats or 1 cup bread crumbs**
**1 can mushroom soup**
**¼ cup onion, chopped**
**½ tsp. salt**
**¼ tsp. pepper**
**½ cup catsup**

Mix all ingredients together. Bake at 350° for hour or until done. Drain off grease. The last 1 minutes of cooking mix together the following and pour over meat loaf:

**¾ cup catsup**
**¼ cup brown sugar**

# SWEET AND SOUR SPARERIBS

This comes from the kitchen of two very good cooks, Pearl Rotschy and Lark Hersey.

3 lbs. spareribs
Salt and Pepper
⅔ cup brown sugar
2 Tbsp. cornstarch
1 tsp. dry mustard
⅔ cup cider vinegar

1 cup canned crushed
   pineapple
½ cup catsup
½ cup water
¼ cup chopped onion
2 Tbsp. soy sauce

Spread ribs in shallow pan. Brown in 425° oven for 20-30 minutes. Drain off fat; sprinkle with salt and pepper. Combine remaining ingredients; cook until thick and glossy. Spoon half of sauce over meat. Reduce heat to 350° and bake 45 minutes. Turn ribs; cover with rest of sauce and bake 30 minutes or until done.

Nothing takes
the place of good
meat on the table!

# MEAT BALLS

From Sharlene Kangas. Very good!

3 lbs. hamburger
1 (12oz.) can evaporated milk
1 cup cracker crumbs
2 eggs
½ tsp. chili powder
½ cup chopped onion

½ tsp. garlic powder (optional)
2 tsp. salt
½ tsp. pepper

SAUCE:
2 cups catsup
1 cup brown sugar
½ tsp. liquid smoke
½ tsp. garlic powder

Mix together. Make into balls. Put on cookie sheet and freeze. When ready to bake, mix sauce ingredients. Put meatballs into large baking pan and cover with sauce. Bake uncovered for 1½ hours at 350°

# LIVER AND ONIONS

My family was raised on liver and onions!

3 slices bacon
¼ cup butter
1 large onion, sliced
1 tsp. sugar
1 lb. calf's liver
½ cup flour
½ tsp. salt
¼ tsp. pepper

Brown bacon until crisp, remove from pan, cool and crumble. Add 2 Tbsp. butter, onion and sugar; cook until onion browns. Remove onion; set aside. Coat liver slices with flour, salt, and pepper. Add remaining butter. Cook liver until done, about 2-3 minutes on each side. Add onions and crumbled bacon.

# FRIED CABBAGE

A good recipe for those early summer cabbages. There is never any left over when I fix this cabbage.

**1 medium head cabbage**
**4 slices bacon**
**¾ cup cream or Half & Half**
**Salt and Pepper to taste**

Chop bacon in small pieces and brown in large fry pan. Cut up cabbage in thin slices and add to fry pan. Salt and pepper well, add a little water, stirring often. After about 5 minutes, add cream or Half & Half. Do not overcook the cabbage, it should be a little crisp.

# BAKED CABBAGE

From Staci Foley.

**1 small cabbage, chopped**
**2 Tbsp. butter**
**2 Tbsp. flour**
**2 cups milk**
**1 cup cheddar cheese, grated**
**1 cup chopped nuts, your**
  **choice**
**Salt and Pepper**

Set oven to 425°. Cook cabbage until almost tender. Melt butter in saucepan, stir in flour and add milk and bring to a boil until thickened. Add cheese and season well. In casserole dish arrange layers with cabbage, sauce, and nuts, finishing with sauce and sprinkling of nuts. Bake for approx. 20 minutes. Top should be golden and bubbling.

# TWICE-BAKED POTATOES

**8 baking potatoes**
**Oil**

Wash and scrub potatoes, dry and rub with oil. Poke potatoes with a fork. Bake in a 400° oven for about 45 minutes or until done. Remove from oven and cool. Cut slices from top of potatoes. Scoop pulp onto bowl. Keep skins intact.

Mix together and add to potato pulp:

**½ cup sour cream**
**1 (3oz.) pkg. cream cheese**
**½ cup butter** (use about 3 Tbsp. for top of potato)
**1 tsp. salt**
**¼ tsp. pepper**

Pile pulp into skins. Drizzle tops of potatoes with butter. Bake in 400° oven until lightly browned.

# A Bucket

Webster says: "A bucket is a round container with a flat bottom and a curved handle, used to hold or carry water, etc."

A bucket is one of the most valuable and used things on a farm.

# OVEN-CRISP SPUDS

Very good and easy to make!

1½-2 lbs. red potatoes
1-2 Tbsp. olive oil
1 tsp. garlic salt
1 tsp. coarse salt
½ tsp. paprika
½ tsp. fresh ground
  pepper

Quarter potatoes, and place in a bowl. Drizzle olive oil over potatoes and toss. Sprinkle garlic salt, salt, pepper, and paprika. Toss to coat well. Arrange potatoes on lightly oiled cookie sheet. Bake at 525° for about 20 minutes. Stir once or twice while cooking. Lastly, raise heat to broil after 20 minutes and broil potatoes until crisp, about 2 minutes.

# CHICKEN-FRIED STEAK

Very good! Always reminds me of days long ago and Uncle Paul and Aunt Margaret's kitchen, as they prepared the best chicken-fried steak!

1 pound top round steak
1 cup fine dry bread crumbs or
  flour
1 tsp. salt
½ tsp. pepper
1 egg, beaten
1 Tbsp. milk

Cut steak into 4 serving-size pieces. Trim fat. Pound meat to ¼" thickness to tenderize. Stir together beaten egg and milk. Dip steak pieces in egg mixture, then coat with crumbs or flour, salt, and pepper. Brown meat in oil on both sides. A dutch oven works great. Reduce heat to low. Add 1 cup milk and 1 cup water. Cover and cook at 325° for 2 hours. Good with a cream gravy.

# POTATO CASSEROLE

One of the most-used recipes from "Taste of Country." This is a hit any time of the year! One of the best cooks we know, my sister-in-law Becky Abernathy, made this and I knew it had to be part of my culinary treasures.

**Cook 6-9 potatoes** (unpeeled)
**¼ cup butter**
**1 cup cream of chicken soup**
**1 pint sour cream**
**1½ cups shredded cheddar cheese**
**½ cup chopped green onions**
**2 Tbsp. melted butter**
**Cornflakes, crushed**

Peel and cube cooked potatoes into casserole dish. Heat ¼ cup butter with onions and soup; add sour cream and cheese. Mix with potatoes. Combine 2 Tbsp. melted butter and cornflakes. Sprinkle over top. Bake at 350° for 45 minutes.

# GARLIC MASHED POTATOES

From Kelli Merriman. No last minute preparation. You will receive rave reviews when you serve this country recipe.

**10 red unpeeled potatoes**
**3 medium cloves garlic**
**TO TASTE: butter, salt, and pepper**
**2 green onions and tops, thinly**
  **sliced**
**3 Tbsp. chicken bouillon granules**
**1 (8oz.) pkg. cream cheese**

Simmer potatoes and peeled whole garlic cloves in water with bouillon. Drain water. Mash or chop garlic cloves and potatoes. Add cream cheese, salt, pepper, and butter. Add milk until desired consistency. Stir in onion. Put potatoes in a crock pot (low heat) an hour before serving.

# FAMOUS FAMILY BAKED BEANS

Five generations of Abernathys have grown, shelled, and dried these unique beans. I have used this recipe for so many years and they are a consistent favorite. You can use white or red beans.

**2 quarts of shell beans or cooked navy beans**
**1 cup brown sugar**
**½ cup butter** (cut into small chunks)
**10 slices bacon**
**Cracked peppercorns**

Mix together in a 9"x 13" enamel pan or pan of choice. Cut bacon slices in 4 pieces and lay on top of beans. Sprinkle with a little more brown sugar and cracked pepper. Bake at 375˚ until bacon is cooked and brown.

# WONDERFUL CORN CASSEROLE

We freeze many, many packages of corn. This is a unique way to serve it, almost like a custard dessert. A meal by itself! Soooo good!

1 pkg. (8oz.) cream cheese, softened
3 eggs, beaten
¼ cup sugar
1 pkg. (small) corn bread/muffin mix

1 can cream-style corn
1 cup milk
3 Tbsp. butter, melted
1 tsp. salt
2½ cups fresh, frozen or canned sweet corn

In a mixing bowl blend cream cheese, eggs, and sugar. Add remaining ingredients and mix well. Pour into a 9"x 13" baking dish. Bake, uncovered, at 350° for 45-50 minutes or until set.

# OLD FASHIONED CORN CAKES

Recipe from my sister Linda Kysar.

1 can whole kernel corn, drained
1 egg
⅓ cup flour

Mix corn and egg in bowl and whip by hand vigorously. Stir in flour and continue to whip until smooth. This should look like pancake batter with corn in it. Drop by large spoonfuls on a hot skillet. Lightly brown on both sides. Salt and pepper to taste.

# CREAMED CORN

What a special treat! Excellent with fresh or frozen corn.

¼ cup butter
2½ cups corn kernels
½ cup milk or Half & Half
1 Tbsp. sugar
½ tsp. salt
¼ tsp. pepper
1 Tbsp. cornstarch

Melt butter in a large skillet over medium heat; stir in corn kernels and milk. Sprinkle with cornstarch, sugar, salt, and pepper. Stir well. Bring mixture to a boil, stirring constantly, reduce heat and simmer about 10 minutes. Serve hot.

# CORN CASSEROLE

Rave reviews from this fantastic recipe! Given by Corinne Abernathy and Kathy Stephenson.

⅓ cup butter
⅓ cup flour
⅛ cup sugar
2 cups Half & Half
1 tsp. salt and pepper
5 cups sweet corn
Parmesan cheese, grated

Stir all ingredients together. Sprinkle top with parmesan cheese. Bake at 350° for 30-45 minutes until golden and bubbly.

A little girl, a father, horses, and a plow. .the smell of fresh dirt, the sweat of horses and man, long rows of farrows, warm dirt squishing between little toes, the wind moving slightly, the sun shining brightly. .all told the story that it was corn planting time on the farm!
                                                                    --Linda Kysar

# PASTIES

Corinne Abernathy says to use any pie crust recipe. She uses butter in the crust for a wonderful flavor.

**FILLING:**
2 lbs. hamburger
12 potatoes, diced
1 turnip, optional
1 medium carrot chopped fine
6-7 carrots, diced

Mix all of the above ingredients together. Divide crust into 10 parts. Roll out each piece on a floured board to the size of an 8-inch pie pan. On half of the dough, place about 3 big spoonfuls of filling. Salt and pepper to taste, and dot with butter. Fold uncovered portion over filled portion, and crimp edges to seal. Cut 2 or 3 small knife slits in top. Pasty is somewhat in the shape of a half moon. Bake 15 minutes at 400°, then lower heat to 350° for 45 minutes. Serves 10-13 people. Very good with catsup.

In upper Michigan, on the Keweenaw Peninsula, is a copper mining area known as "The Copper Country." Copper has been mined here since the ancient times. The copper is pure native copper. This is the only place in the world where it was mined commercially.

Most of the grandparents of the people I grew up with were from "the old country" (i.e., England, Finland, Sweden, Croatia, Italy, France). Cornwall, England was highly represented as the Cornish had been expert miners for centuries, mostly mining tin. The tin mining in Cornwall was dying out, and when the Cornish heard of the copper mining opening up, they came in droves. Wherever they go they are known as "Cousin Jacks." The story is if the mines needed new help, they always had a cousin Jack that came to work.

The Cornish men got the jobs as bosses as they were the only newcomers who spoke English. They brought with them their Cornish pasty, a juicy meat and vegetable mixture enclosed in a pastry crust. If you insist on being genuinely Cornish, you use only rutabaga as the vegetable. In this day, everyone's pasty is as individual as everyone's bread. Even as little children, we always had a cup of tea with our pasty, English style, a custom my mother learned from the Cornish.

My sister cross-stitched a picture of the typical lunch pail of the miner. In the bottom went the hot tea, which kept the pasty warm. In the upper part went the pasty. I heard recently that some of the old timers made the pasty half meat and vegetable and the other half fruit.

-CORINNE KYSAR

# PASTY

From Corinne Kysar. Corinne says she uses pork sausage for lean pork.

**2 cups lean ground beef**
**¾ cup lean pork**
**3 cups potatoes, diced**
**1 medium onion, diced**
**1 medium rutabaga,**
   (can be diced or grated)
**2 tsp. salt**
**Plenty of pepper**
**Butter**

Combine all ingredients. Use your own crust recipe. Use a luncheon plate for a guide when cutting pastry out for pasty. Place ¾ cup of mixture on lower half of circle and dot with butter. Fold top over and crimp edges to seal. Pierce top crust with fork. Bake at 425° for 15 minutes, then 350° for 45 minutes.

Corinne says, "a true Cornish pasty has no carrots in it." In place of potatoes, use frozen hash browns, a wonderful tip from Alice Ek.

## OVEN CLAMS

My sister-in-law Beth Malinowski gave me this wonderful recipe.

Dip **razor clams** in beaten eggs, then coat with **Ritz Cracker** crumbs. Lay clams on greased cookie sheet. **Salt** lightly and drizzle with **melted butter**. Bake in hot oven at 525° for 10-12 minutes. We do the best Zucchini the same way, only cut heat to 500° until brown, about 12 minutes.

## FRIED CLAMS

Oh, what a treat. Sonny and Jack love to dig them and I enjoy frying clams.

**Vegetable oil**
**¾ cup flour**
**1 tsp. salt**
**¼ tsp. pepper**
**3 dozen clams**
**3-4 eggs, beaten**
**½ cup milk**
**1-2 cups cracker crumbs or bread crumbs**

Heat oil (1-1½") in fry pan or dutch oven. Mix flour, salt, and pepper. Cut clams into about 4 pieces. Coat clams with flour mixture, dip in egg and milk, then coat with crumbs. Fry about 2 minutes or until golden brown. Drain on paper towels.

---

The steelhead can hurtle into the air a split second after he is hooked, and flash hugely out in the murk, like the sword Excalibur thrust up from the depths—at once a gleaming prize and symbol of battle.   - PAUL O'NEIL

---

## JEROD'S BBQ STEELHEAD

My oldest grandson, Jerod Esteb, has mastered the fish as well as the fishing pole! Here is his fabulous recipe.

Filet large steelhead or salmon length-wise into 2 halves. Apply liberally in order given:

**Salt**
**Cracked lemon pepper**
**Mayonnaise**
**Brown sugar**
**Concentrated lime juice**

Place skin side down on grill. (Fish can be placed skin side down on foil or cookie sheet before grilling.) Cook at medium temperature until juices run clear— approximately 30 minutes.

# DEEP FRIED FISH

We use salmon, halibut, steelhead or whatever is available. This is our favorite way to fix fish. We usually have baked spuds and onion rings when I cook deep fried fish.

**2-inch chunks of fish**
**1 cup milk**
**2 eggs**
**Flour**
**Cracker crumbs**
**Vegetable oil**
**Salt and Pepper**
**Tartar sauce and lemon**

*I also do fresh oysters with this recipe!*

Filet fish into 2 inch chunks. Roll out crackers to make a good size dish of crumbs. Beat eggs and add milk. Dip chunks of fish in flour, then egg and milk mixture, last roll in cracker crumbs. Fry at 375° in vegetable oil covering fish...until golden brown, about 5 minutes. Remove from oil. Salt and pepper. These tasty morsels are also good cold in lunches.

# ONION RINGS

Be prepared with several onions – these rings go fast! Soooo crunchy and tasty.

Peel onion. Slice onion into ¼ inch rings and separate. Put rings in flour, then into egg and milk, lastly back into the flour. Gently place in hot vegetable oil. Fry until golden brown. Always place deep fried foods on paper towels to absorb grease.

# GARDEN FRESH POLE BEANS

Old time eating!

**2 pounds pole beans**
**3 bacon slices**
**1 cup water**
**1 tsp. salt**
**½ tsp. pepper**
**1 Tbsp. sugar**

Snap beans in half or desired size pieces. Set aside. Cook bacon in a skillet until crisp. Reserve bacon grease. Crumble bacon and set aside. Add water, salt, sugar, and pepper to kettle; bring to a full boil over high heat. Add beans, cover, reduce heat, and cook 15 minutes or to desired doneness. Sprinkle with crumbled bacon and drippings.

# SPAGHETTI PIE

xcellent!  From Sharlene Kangas

**COMBINE: (1ST LAYER)**

½ lbs. browned hamburger
tsp. oregano, dried
tsp. basil, dried
(32oz.) jar spaghetti sauce
0oz. cooked spaghetti noodles

**COMBINE: (2ND LAYER)**

(24oz.) carton cottage cheese
beaten eggs
tsp. salt
½ tsp. pepper
½ cup parmesan cheese

**COMBINE: (3RD LAYER)**

lb. shredded mozzarella
heese

ayer twice, using ½ of each combination
wo times.  Bake covered for 20 minutes
t 350˚.  Let stand for 15 minutes.

# ZUCCHINI BAKE

This recipe is from Elaine Sarkinen and she says it is her family's favorite way to fix zucchini.

**1 large zucchini**
**½ cup grated cheese**
**12 small crackers, crushed**
**1 small onion, chopped**
**2 eggs, beaten**
**Garlic salt, optional**
**Salt to taste**

Peel and cook zucchini until tender; drain and mash.  Combine all ingredients and mix well.  Turn into buttered baking dish and bake uncovered for 45 minutes at 350˚.  Also can be baked in microwave for approx. 15 minutes.

# SPINACH PIE

From Kathleen Rinta. Kathleen says, "I always use Lawry's Seasoned Salt.  I tried another brand once and it's just not the same.  My sister-in-law, who does not like spinach, always takes at least a second helping!"

**2 (10oz.) boxes frozen, chopped**
   **spinach**
**1 (16oz.) carton small curd cottage**
   **cheese**
**3 large eggs, beaten**
**1-2 tsp. Lawry's Seasoned Salt**
**¼ tsp. pepper**
**Dash of salt** (optional)
**¼ -½ cup grated cheddar cheese**

Thaw spinach; squeeze very dry.  Mix spinach, cottage cheese, eggs, seasoned salt, pepper, and salt together well.  Pour into greased 8" pie pan or 8" x 8" square baking pan.  Bake in preheated 350˚ oven for 25-30 minutes or until a toothpick inserted in the middle comes out almost clean.  Sprinkle cheese over the top and cover loosely with foil until it melts.  Cool for 5-10 minutes before cutting into serving size pieces.

# WINTER ROOT VEGETABLES

From Kelli Merriman. This recipe is so good in the fall. I added chunks of sweet potatoes and we really like it.

2 pounds small red potatoes, quartered

1 pound brussel sprouts

½ pound parsnips, peeled and julienned

½ pound carrots, cut into chunks

2 turnips, peeled and cut into chunks

½ cup butter

2 Tbsp. prepared horseradish (optional)

2 Tbsp. cider vinegar

2 Tbsp. snipped fresh dill or 2½ tsp. dried dill weed

½ tsp. salt

¼ tsp. pepper

Cook vegetables separately until tender. Melt butter, stir in remaining ingredients, toss to coat. Can be kept warm in a crock pot.

# MY FAVORITE SWEET POTATOES

For generations my relatives have been making sweet potatoes like this.

Cook your sweet potatoes; cool, then peel them. Cut into pieces, Place them in a baking dish. Sprinkle with salt and pepper. We add the amount of brown sugar that we like over the tops of the sweet potatoes. Now comes the secret of goodness! Pour whipping cream about 1 to 2 inches deep over top and dot with real butter. Bake at 350° about 30 minutes or until cream bubbles up and makes a sauce.

# ROAST TURKEY WITH CORN BREAD STUFFING

**10-12 lb. bird**

Heat oven to 325°. Fill wish bone neck area of turkey lightly with stuffing. Fold skin under. Fill body cavity lightly. (Do not pack. Stuffing will expand while cooking.) Spoon remaining stuffing into small greased glass casserole; cover and refrigerate. Place casserole in the oven with turkey during the last 30 minutes. Place turkey, breast side up, into a Reynolds oven bag that has been floured. Roast 3½ to 4 hours or until meat thermometer registers 185°. Let stand about 20 minutes before carving.

# CORN BREAD STUFFING

2 boxes corn bread stuffing, seasoned
2 cups finely cut celery
1 medium onion, chopped
½ cup butter
4 eggs, beaten
1 tsp. salt
¼ tsp. sage
½ tsp. pepper
2 (14oz.) cans chicken broth (stir in enough water to moisten stuffing)

Saute onion and celery in butter. Toss and mix together with corn bread and the rest of ingredients. Add browned and crumbled Jimmy Dean sausage if desired.

# BROILED TURKEY SANDWICHES

For that leftover turkey. Handy, happy, and hearty lunch special.

Make sandwiches on toasted bread. On inside slices of bread, spread generously with cranberry sauce and cream cheese. Top with turkey slices and then place a thin slice of cheese of your choice on top of turkey. Place under broiler until cheese is melted. Serve warm.

89

# SPARERIBS WITH APPLES AND SAUERKRAUT

Enthusiastically received if you like sauerkraut!

Arrange sauerkraut over the bottom of a covered roasting pan. Put cored apples, (the cavities filled with brown sugar) down in a bed of sauerkraut. Arrange spareribs over all. Season with salt and pepper. Roast at 350˚ for 1½ hours.

# MACARONI AND CHEESE BALLS

Lucy Cahoon mastered these unique delicious macaroni and cheese balls. WOW! She also made the macaroni and cheese.

**Shape ½-cup portions of macaroni and cheese into balls. Roll balls in milk and then seasoned Italian breadcrumbs. May add seasoning of choice. Deep fry in vegetable oil until brown, approximately 2 minutes.**

*Age is something that doesn't matter, unless you are cheese.*

-BILLIE BURKE

# MACARONI AND CHEESE

Everyone loves this macaroni and cheese. It's creamy and easy to make. A terrific potluck casserole. Very rich and yummy.

1 (7oz.) pkg. elbow macaroni
6 Tbsp. butter, divided
3 Tbsp. flour
2½ cups milk (I use part canned)
1 (8oz.) pkg. cream cheese
3 cups cheddar cheese, grated
½ tsp. salt
½ tsp. pepper
1 cup dry bread crumbs

Cook macaroni until tender as directed on package. Melt 4 Tbsp. butter in saucepan. Stir in flour until smooth. Gradually add milk; bring to boil, stirring constantly. Add cream cheese and 2 cups of cheddar cheese, salt, and pepper. Stir on low heat until cheeses are melted and smooth. Drain and rinse macaroni and mix cheese mixture into it. Transfer to casserole dish or 9" x 13" pan. Melt remaining 2 Tbsp. of butter and add bread crumbs. Sprinkle remaining 1 cup cheddar cheese on top. Lastly, add buttered bread crumbs. Bake uncovered at 400° for 20-25 minutes or until golden brown.

# CREAM CAN DINNER

From Barb Creel in Colorado.  A real crowd pleaser!

Wash cream can really well.  Be sure there are no holes or rust in can.  Place metal strainer (the small fold out kind) in bottom of can.

Add:

**6 pkgs. Polska Kielbasa, cut into quarters**
**25 peeled whole potatoes**
**10 peeled onions, cut in half**
**15 ears corn, shucked and cleaned - break in half**
**5 heads of cabbage, cut in quarters**
**1 gallon water**
**Salt and Pepper to taste**

Set lid ajar on can.  Do not put on tight.  Cook outside on propane burner or campfire.  Bring to full boil, lower heat to medium-low.  Simmer 45 minutes.  Pour into a clean galvanized tub.

# IMPOSSIBLE TACO PIE

From Beth Malinowski. She says, "The green chilies are optional."

2 lbs. ground beef
½ cup onion, chopped
1 pkg. taco seasoning
1 can green chilies, drained
2 cups milk
1 cup Bisquick
4 eggs
2 tomatoes
2 cups cheese of your choice, shredded
Sour cream

Heat oven to 400°. Grease 10" quiche dish or pie plate. Brown beef along with onion over medium heat until beef is cooked; drain. Stir in seasoning mix. Spread in plate; sprinkle with chilies. Beat milk, Bisquick, and eggs until smooth, 15 seconds on high in blender or 1 minute with hand beater. Pour into pie plate. Bake 25 minutes. Top with tomatoes; sprinkle with cheese. Bake 8-10 minutes longer or until knife inserted in center comes out clean. Cool 5 minutes. Serve with sour cream. Very good! I replace ¼ cup of Bisquick with corn meal for added flavor.

# ROASTED CARROTS

I tasted these yummy carrots at Dotty Halberg's house and I knew with the first bite that I must have the recipe!

2 lbs. carrots, peeled and cut into 2½ inch strips
3 Tbsp. melted butter
2 Tbsp. brown sugar
½ tsp. salt
½ tsp. pepper

Heat oven to 475°. Heat baking sheet in oven for at least 8 minutes. Cut carrots into strips. Mix together butter, sugar, salt, and pepper. Toss carrots with butter mixture. Remove pan from oven; place carrots in a single layer on hot baking sheet. Roast carrots for 15 minutes. Toss carrots and continue to roast for another 3 minutes or until tender.

Good communication is as stimulating as black coffee and just as hard to sleep after.

–ANNE MORROW LINDBERGH

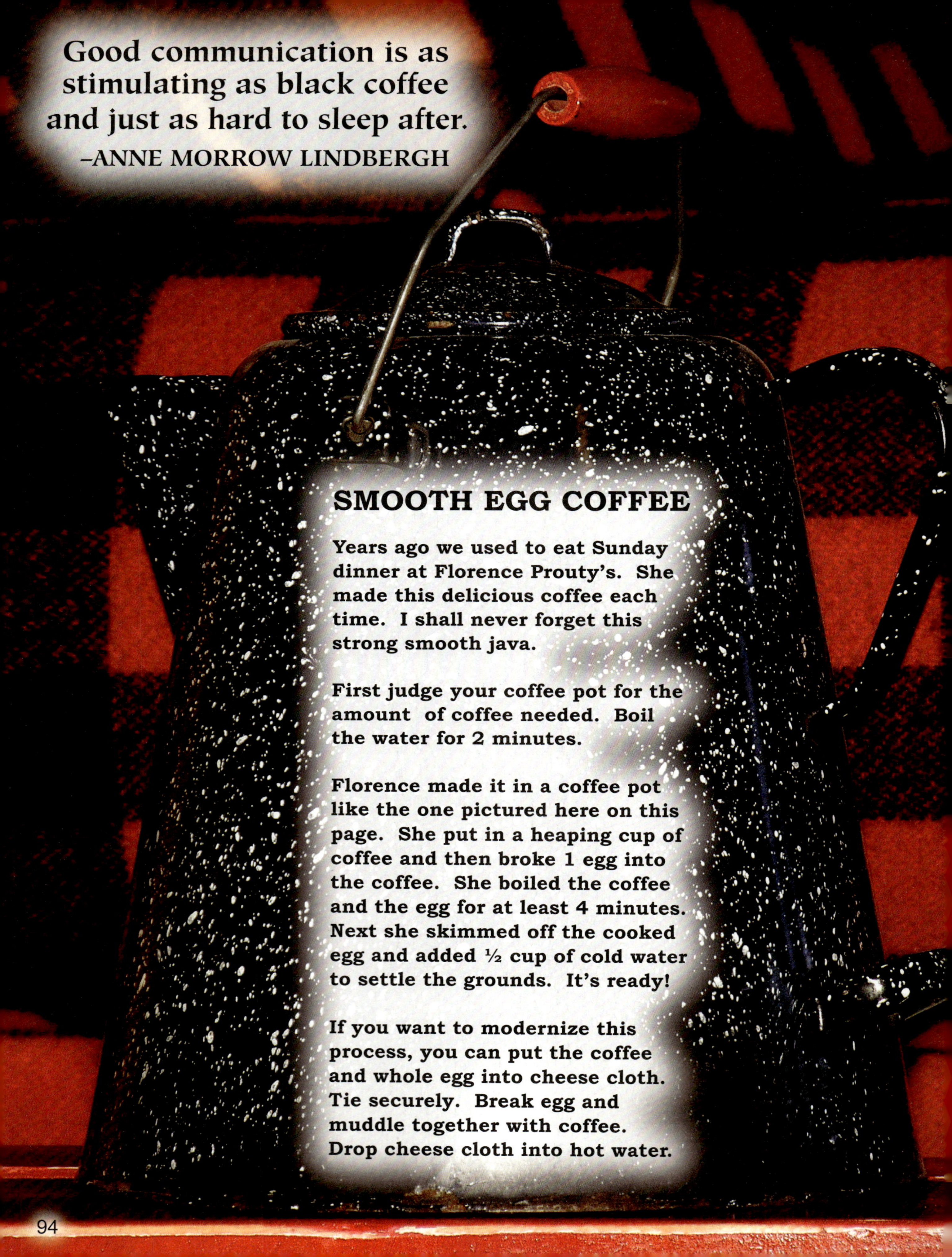

## SMOOTH EGG COFFEE

Years ago we used to eat Sunday dinner at Florence Prouty's. She made this delicious coffee each time. I shall never forget this strong smooth java.

First judge your coffee pot for the amount of coffee needed. Boil the water for 2 minutes.

Florence made it in a coffee pot like the one pictured here on this page. She put in a heaping cup of coffee and then broke 1 egg into the coffee. She boiled the coffee and the egg for at least 4 minutes. Next she skimmed off the cooked egg and added ½ cup of cold water to settle the grounds. It's ready!

If you want to modernize this process, you can put the coffee and whole egg into cheese cloth. Tie securely. Break egg and muddle together with coffee. Drop cheese cloth into hot water.

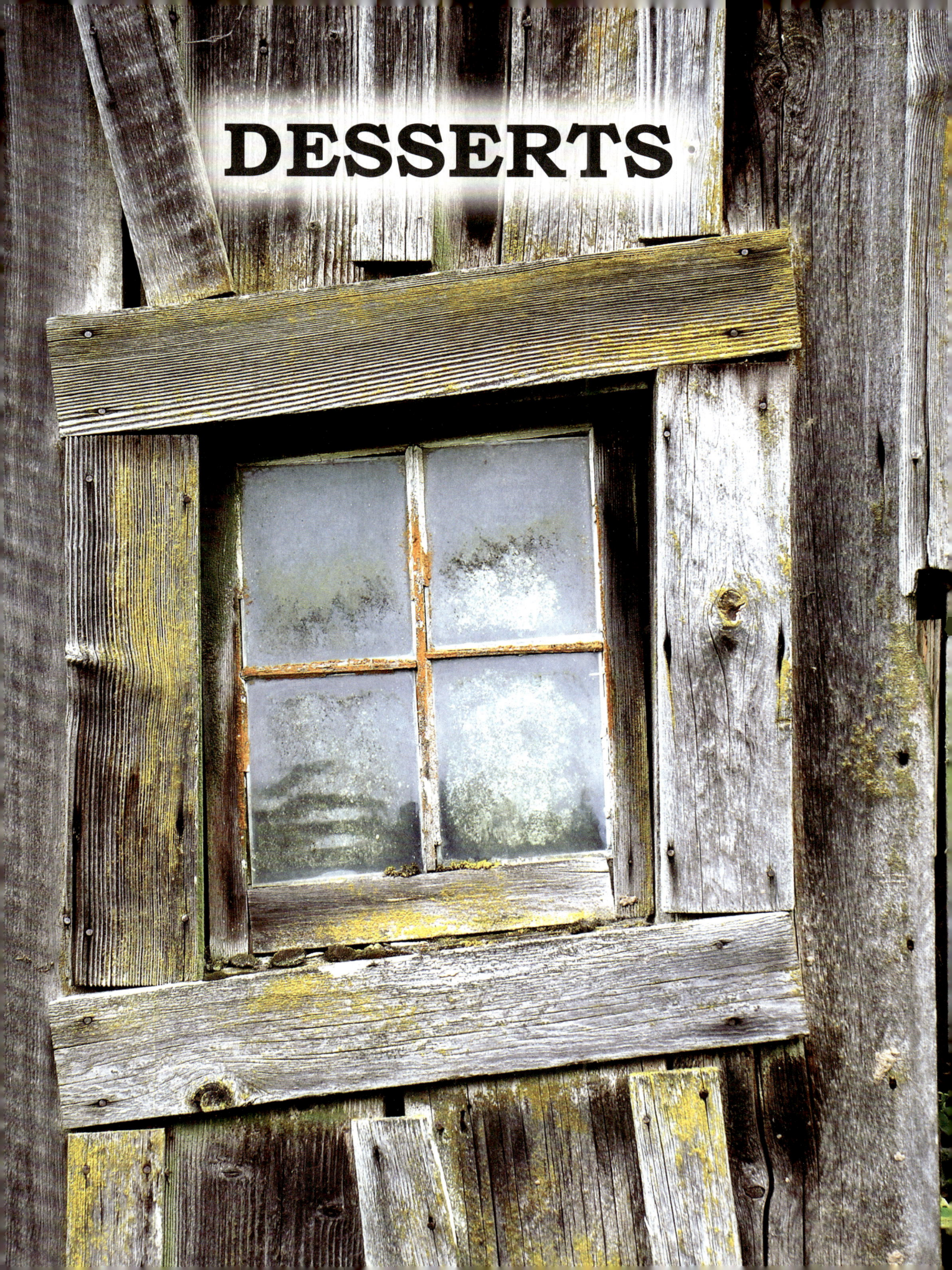

# DESSERTS

# SWEET RICE

A delicious pudding that I have been making for a long time. For a richer pudding, I sometimes use part evaporated milk. My cousin, Lark Hersey, passed this on to me.

¾ cup uncooked rice
2 cups water
3 cups milk
4 Tbsp. butter
1 tsp. salt

Mix rice water, milk, butter, and salt. Bring to boil, then set on low burner for about 30 minutes with lid on kettle.

2 eggs
1 cup sugar
1 tsp. vanilla

Beat eggs and add sugar. Put a little of the hot rice mixture, slowly, into egg mixture, stirring the whole time. Put all together in the kettle; add vanilla. Turn off stove, put lid back on kettle. Let set until thick; spoon into dessert dishes.

# FRAN'S CUSTARD

We take this custard to the sick, usually adding mo[re] eggs.

3 or 4 eggs, slightly beaten
¼ cup sugar
Pinch of salt
2 tsp. vanilla
Powdered milk

Mix enough powdered milk following directio[ns] on box, with hot water, to make 2 cups, the[n] add to above mixture. Pour into 6 custard cup[s] and set in pan of hot water . Sprinkle top with [a] little nutmeg and cinnamo[n.] Bake just until table kni[fe] inserted inch fro[m] edge com[es] out clea[n] 35-40 min[utes] at 325˚.

## PRUNE TARTS

This recipe is from Marie Rotschy.

Mix like pie crust:

**4 cups flour**
**¼ cup sugar**
**1 lb. butter**

Add and chill:

**2 beaten eggs**
**½ cup milk**

Cook over medium heat, until they are falling apart:

**2 lbs. pitted prunes or apricots**
**1-2 Tbsp. sugar**

Roll out small amounts of dough to pie crust thickness. Cut dough into small squares (about 2 inches). Put a spoonful of fruit in center and fold opposite corners together or cut corners ½ inch up and fold every other corner to center. Sprinkle with sugar and bake at 375° for 10-15 minutes. Do not overbake.

# DANISH ALMOND PUFFS

You'll be thankful for this one.

1 cup plus 1 Tbsp. butter
2 cups flour
1 tsp. almond flavoring
3 eggs
2 cups powdered sugar
4 Tbsp. cream
1 tsp. vanilla
⅛ tsp. salt
2 Tbsp. cold water
1 cup boiling water

## PASTRY:

Cut ½ cup butter into 1 cup flour until mixture resembles coarse meal; add 2 Tbsp. cold water and stir until well blended. Divide dough in half; press each half into 3" x 12" rectangle on ungreased baking sheet. Place 1 cup boiling water and ½ cup butter in sauce pan; bring to boil. Add almond flavoring; remove from heat. Stir in remaining flour; add eggs one at a time, beating well. Spread over pastry rectangles. Bake at 400° for 50 minutes. Combine remaining butter, powdered sugar, cream, vanilla, and salt; beat until smooth. Frost hot pastry. I always drizzle raspberry or strawberry jam down the center of rectangle. Wonderful with ground nuts.

"Impatient peop[le]
water their miseri[es]
and hoe up the
comforts."

–Old Home Book 19[__]

# HEIDI'S COCONUT CREAM PUFFS

This is an excellent recipe from my daughter, Heidi Esteb.

1 cup water
½ cup butter
1 cup flour
4 eggs

COCOA FROSTING:
2 cups powdered sugar
¼ cup unsweetened chocolate
3 Tbsp. butter
3-4 Tbsp. hot water

Bring water and butter to rolling boil. Stir in flour, stirring vigorously over low heat until ball forms, about 1 minute. Remove from heat. Beat in eggs all at once until smooth. Drop dough by scant ¼ cupfuls about 3 inches apart onto ungreased cookie sheet. Bake at 400° until puffed and golden, about 35 minutes. Cool away from draft. Cut off tops; pull out any filaments of dough. Fill puffs with your favorite coconut cream filling. Replace tops. Frost with cocoa frosting; sprinkle coconut on top.

Small Ronald having arrived at the story-loving age, his mother read to him every night. One evening, she was unable to find the book, so entertained him with an account of her girlhood on the farm. Ronald's eyes grew bigger and bigger as she told of her wading in the pond, going berry picking, and riding a real, live horse. "Gee mom," he sighed wistfully, "I sure wish I'd met you earlier!"

- WEBB B. GARRISON

# LEMON PUFF PILLOW BUNS

So good! From my daughter-in-law Tina Gillette.

3¼ cups flour
1 Tbsp. yeast
¾ cup milk
6 Tbsp. butter
¼ cup sugar
1 tsp. salt
2 eggs

1 tsp. grated lemon peel
4 (3oz.) pkgs. cream cheese, softened
3 Tbsp. sugar
1 egg yolk
1 tsp. vanilla
1 beaten egg white

In large mixing bowl, combine 1½ cups flour and all of the yeast. In saucepan heat milk, butter, ¼ cup sugar, and salt just until warm, stirring constantly, until butter is melted. Add to dry mixture in mixing bowl. Add 2 eggs and lemon peel. Beat at low speed on electric mixer for ½ minute, scraping sides of bowl constantly. Beat 3 minutes at high speed. By hand, stir in remaining flour. Cover bowl lightly; refrigerate at least 4 hours or overnight. When ready to shape blend together cream cheese, 3 Tbsp. sugar egg yolk, and vanilla. Divide dough into quarters. On generously floured board, roll each portion into a 12x8-inch rectangle (keep remaining dough refrigerated). Cut into six 4-inch squares. Place about 1 Tbsp. cream cheese mixture in center of each; bring opposite corners to the center and pinch to seal. Place two inches apart on greased baking sheet. Brush with beaten egg white. Let rise uncovered, in warm place until half again as large (20-30 minutes). Bake at 400° until done, about 10 minutes. Makes 24.

# 1-2-3 LAYER DESSERT

This recipe hails from Michigan. My mother made it so many times we all call it "Lucy's Luscious."

## NUT CRUST:

**½ cup butter**
**1 cup nuts**
**1¼ cups flour**

Mix and press into 9"x 13" pan. Bake until light brown, about 15 minutes.

## LAYER#1:

**1 cup powdered sugar**
**1 (8oz.) pkg. cream cheese**
**½ carton Cool Whip**

Mix together and spoon onto cooled crust.

## LAYER#2:

**Instant butterscotch pudding (3oz.)**
Follow directions on pkg. using 1½ cups milk. Spread on top of layer#1.

## LAYER#3:

**Instant chocolate pudding (3oz.)**
**Follow directions on pkg. using 1½ cups milk** Spread on top of layer#2.

On top of layer #3, put rest of Cool Whip; sprinkle with nuts. Chill and cut into squares.

# CRUNCHY CREAM DESSERT SQUARES

Many have enjoyed this dessert made many times by my sister-in-law, Becky Abernathy.

**1 cup flour**
**¼ cup sugar**
**½ cup butter**
**1 cup coconut**
**1 pkg. (3oz.) vanilla pudding**
**1¾ cups milk**
**1 cup whipping cream**
**2 Tbsp. sugar**
**½ tsp. vanilla**

In ungreased 9" square pan, combine first 4 ingredients until crumbly. Bake at 350°, stirring occasionally, until golden brown (crunchy texture). Cool. In large bowl, whip cream until thickened; blend in sugar and vanilla. Reserve 1 cup cooled crumb mixture; press remaining crumbs over bottom of pan. Spoon pudding evenly over crumbs. Top with whipped cream. Sprinkle with remaining crumbs. Chill 2-3 hours before serving.

# APPLE CRISP

From Corrine Abernathy.

**6 medium apples, cored, peeled, and sliced.**
**1 cup brown sugar**
**¾ cup flour**

**¾ cup oatmeal**
**1 tsp. cinnamon**
**½ cup butter** (<u>not</u> melted)

Mix crust mixture all together and crumble over apples. Bake at 350° for 35 minutes. Serve warm!

# SODA CRACKER TORTE

I have one sister.  Words cannot express my feeling about my sister.  She's always there when I need her. She's my friend. Linda Kysar adds this yummy dessert to our family gatherings.

**6 egg whites**
**¾ tsp. cream of tartar**
**2 cups sugar**
**2 cups crushed soda crackers**
**¾ cup nuts**
**2 tsp. vanilla**
**2 cups whipping cream**
**1 can cherry pie filling**

Beat egg whites until frothy, add cream of tartar, then gradually add sugar.  Beat until stiff.  Fold in crushed crackers, nuts, and vanilla.  Spread in greased 9"x 13" glass baking dish.  Bake at 350° for 25 minutes.  Cool. Whip cream, spread over top and spoon pie filling over whipped cream.  Chill.

# JELL-O FILLED ROLL-UP

From Lyudmila Palamaryuk. Make finger JELL-O deep enough to get a long 1 inch square cube to put in the middle of filling.

Mix together very well:

**6 eggs**
**½ cup sugar**

Sift together:

**1 cup flour**
**1 tsp. baking soda**

Mix dry ingredients into eggs and sugar mixture. Divide dough into two 9"x 13" jelly roll pans. Bake cakes at 350° for 20-25 minutes until cakes are done.

**CREAM FILLING:**

Mix all together:

**1 (8oz.) pkg. cream cheese**
**½ cup butter, softened**
**1 (16oz.) Cool Whip**
**½ cup powdered sugar**

Spread filling on cakes, place strip of firm JELL-O on center of filling. Frost with whipped cream and decorate as desired.

# STRAWBERRY BAVARIAN CREAM PUDDING

We get this dessert at the Oak Tree Restaurant. It is not that hard to make.

½ cup sugar
1 envelope unflavored gelatin
¼ tsp. salt
2¼ cups milk
3 eggs, slightly beaten
1 cup whipping cream
1 tsp. vanilla
¼ cup slivered roasted almonds

Mix together first five ingredients and cook over medium heat, stirring constantly, just until mixture comes to a boil. Cool and fold in whipping cream, whipped stiff with vanilla. Chill until firm. Spoon into small dishes and serve with fresh or frozen strawberries on top. Delicious sprinkled with slivered, roasted almonds.

# STRAWBERRY SHORTCAKE

An old time American favorite!

Sift dry ingredients:
**2 cups flour**
**2 Tbsp. sugar**
**3 tsp. baking powder**
**1 tsp. salt**

Cut in with pastry blender:
**⅓ cup shortening**

Stir in:
**1 cup milk or Half & Half**
(Half & Half makes dough richer)

Spread dough into a greased round pan. Bake at 400° for 20-30 minutes. Cut round shortcake into two layers. Place first cooled layer on dish and cover with whipped cream and sugared berries. Top with second layer. Serve warm with more whipped cream or ice cream. Any good recipe for biscuit dough may be used. Sometimes when we are in a hurry, we use Bisquick.

# REMEMBERING THE APPLE MAN

I was raised in the big city of Minneapolis and pursued a career in art. While working a year abroad at an advertising agency in Helsinki, Finland, I met an intriguing traveler named Pierre. I soon learned that this gentle man from Yacolt, Washington had a strong faith in God and a huge heart. I was 24. He was 33, a high school French and English teacher, an educated man who loved word games, poetry, writing, storytelling, and.....farming. Interesting combination: the country life complete with orchards filled with fruit, rows of grapes, vegetable garden, pigs, cattle, and chickens. A day job filled with intellect, and then home to the farm.

His dreams were many. I was so fortunate to become his wife, helping him to fulfill his dreams for 29 years. We ran a retail nursery specializing in fruit trees, but most of all—apple trees. He wanted everyone to be able to grow their own edible landscaping. Since that wasn't really possible, we built a cooler in 1990 and sold year around so everyone could afford lots of fruit: peaches, pears, cherries, blueberries, but most of all—apples. Our commercial cider press could make 50 gallons a squeezing and people flocked to buy it. Pierre was an apple man to the core!

He was a good cook and taught me how to can. We kept a record book of everything we preserved. Our orchards and gardens expanded. Everything I know about growing I learned from him. His gentle tutoring and loving encouragement made the transition from city girl to country farmer girl a fulfilling journey.

God gave us 8 children—the last two a grand bonus set of twins when I was 43 and he was 52. He said, "Just think, Mother, a girl for you and a boy for me to help us in our old age!" It wasn't meant to be. Cancer took Pierre's life at age 63, but not his spirit. We are all, including the 12 grandkids, reaping the legacy he sowed.

Pierre's greatest talent was not that he belonged to two careers, but that he encouraged everything and everyone to grow—his family, his students, his plants, and me, his city bred wife. He saw the best in all, even if they didn't see it in themselves, most especially in me. He saw that the city girl had a country heart, and he set that heart free.

-Marilyn  Rotschy

# CHERRY CHEESECAKE

Want a quick dessert?  Then this is it!

**2½ cups graham cracker crumbs,
    crushed**
**¼ cup sugar**
**½ cup butter, melted**
**2 (8oz.) pkgs. cream cheese, softened**
**1 can sweetened condensed milk**
**½ cup lemon juice**
**1-2 cans cherry pie filling**

Add sugar and butter to crushed crackers.  Mix well and pat into 9"x 13" pan.  Bake at 350° for 10 minutes.  Cool.  Beat together cream cheese, condensed milk, and lemon juice until smooth.  Pour over cooled crust.  Top with pie filling.  Refrigerate at least 2 hours before serving.

# DANE'S BREAD PUDDING

**2 eggs**
**6 cups whole milk**
**2 Tbsp. vanilla**
**About 2 Tbsp. cinnamon**
**1½ cups raisins**
**1⅓ cups sugar**
**Enough stale or fresh sliced bread until**
**most of the mixture is soaked up**
**1 pound cake, dried and cubed**

Mix all ingredients well, except for bread and pound cake.  Pour milk mixture over pound cake and bread.  Bake at 350° in 9"x 13" pan just until light brown on top.  An option would be to add diced sweet apples.

Dane Hersey tells us, "Around Thanksgiving and Christmas time my teacher from the Skills Center said, 'Dane, invent something good to serve this season in the restaurant.'  It took a while to perfect, but I did it.  I thought a good bread pudding would do the trick and it sold like hot cakes!  I would make pound cake first and cube it,  then dry it out and mix it with a little bread for better pudding.  I also make a caramel sauce to go over the top."

# CARAMEL SAUCE

**1 cup sugar**
**¼ cup water**
**1 Tbsp. lemon juice**
**2 Tbsp. butter**
**1 cup whipping cream**

Bring the sugar, water, and lemon juice to a boil.  Reduce heat to medium.  Cook until sugar is dissolved and mixture is a golden amber.  Stir in butter; add cream.  Remove from heat and serve over bread pudding.

# HOT FUDGE PUDDING

A favorite at our home for years. The rich pudding on the bottom of the cake makes this popular. Spoon into bowls and serve with whipped cream or ice cream.

1 cup flour
2 tsp. baking powder
¼ tsp. salt
¾ cup sugar
2 Tbsp. cocoa

Stir in:
½ cup milk
2 Tbsp. butter
1 cup chopped nuts

**TOPPING:**
1 cup brown sugar

Mix together with:
¼ cup cocoa

Mix sifted dry ingredients with milk and melted butter. Add nuts. Pour into greased 9 inch square pan. Sprinkle with topping. Lastly, pour 1¾ cups hot water over entire cake. Bake at 350° about 45 minutes.

# OLD FASHIONED ICE CREAM

Makes 4 quarts.

4 eggs
2½ cups sugar
5 cups milk
4 cups whipping cream
3 tsp. vanilla
½ tsp. salt

In large mixing bowl, beat eggs until foamy. Gradually add sugar; beat until thickened. Add cream, vanilla, and salt and mix thoroughly. Pour into can inside ice cream maker. Add milk to fill line on can. Freeze as directed. Vanilla recipes may be varied. Peaches, bananas, strawberries, or other desired fruit may be added. We suggest 1 cup fruit per quart of ice cream.

When ice cream is set, pack freezer with additional ice and rock salt. Let stand 1 hour before serving.

Oh my, the memories of homemade ice cream! Always a part of the Fourth of July. It is a very rewarding accomplishment! Of course now, everyone uses an electric ice cream maker.

MORTON®

ICE CREAM SALT

Rock Salt For Ice Cream & Cooling

4 LB NET WT. (1.8 kg)

# BUTTER PECAN ICE CREAM

My favorite!  Makes 2 quarts.

**1½ cups brown sugar**
**1 cup milk**
**½ tsp. salt**
**4 large eggs, beaten**
**2 Tbsp. butter**

Cook first 3 ingredients in the top of double boiler until sugar dissolves. Gradually stir in a small amount of hot mixture into eggs; add to remaining hot mixture, stirring constantly until mixture thickens.  Remove from heat.  Stir in 2 Tbsp. of butter. Cool.

Add to above cooled mixture:
**2 cups whole milk**
**2 tsp. vanilla**
**2 cups whipping cream**
**1 cup toasted pecans, finely chopped**

Pour mixture into freezer.  Follow instructions on how to freeze ice cream using rock salt. This recipe may be doubled.

"War is an ugly thing but not the ugliest of things; the decayed and degraded state of mind that thinks nothing is worth fighting for is far worse."

-CW2 McClellan, Jonah U.S. Army
Black Hawk pilot deploying to Afghanistan Jan/08
Currently stationed at Fort Campbell, Kentucky Sept. 11th, 2007

4TH YEAR SERVING AMERICA

# APPLE DUMPLINGS

You'll get compliments on these wonderful dumplings.

Make pie crust for double crust pie. Will make 6 dumplings. Roll out crust to about ⅛ inch thick. Cut crust into 8 inch squares. Peel and remove cores of 6 tart apples.

**SYRUP:**
1 cup sugar
2 cups water
3 Tbsp. butter
½ tsp. cinnamon

**FILLING:**
¾ cup sugar
2 tsp. cinnamon
3 Tbsp. butter

Boil syrup for 3 minutes. Place apple on each square of crust. Fill cavity of each apple with filling and dab of butter. Bring opposite points of crust up over apple. Overlap and seal. Place carefully, a little apart in a 9"x 13" baking dish. Pour hot syrup around dumplings. Bake at 375° for about 45 minutes. You may add chopped pecans to syrup.

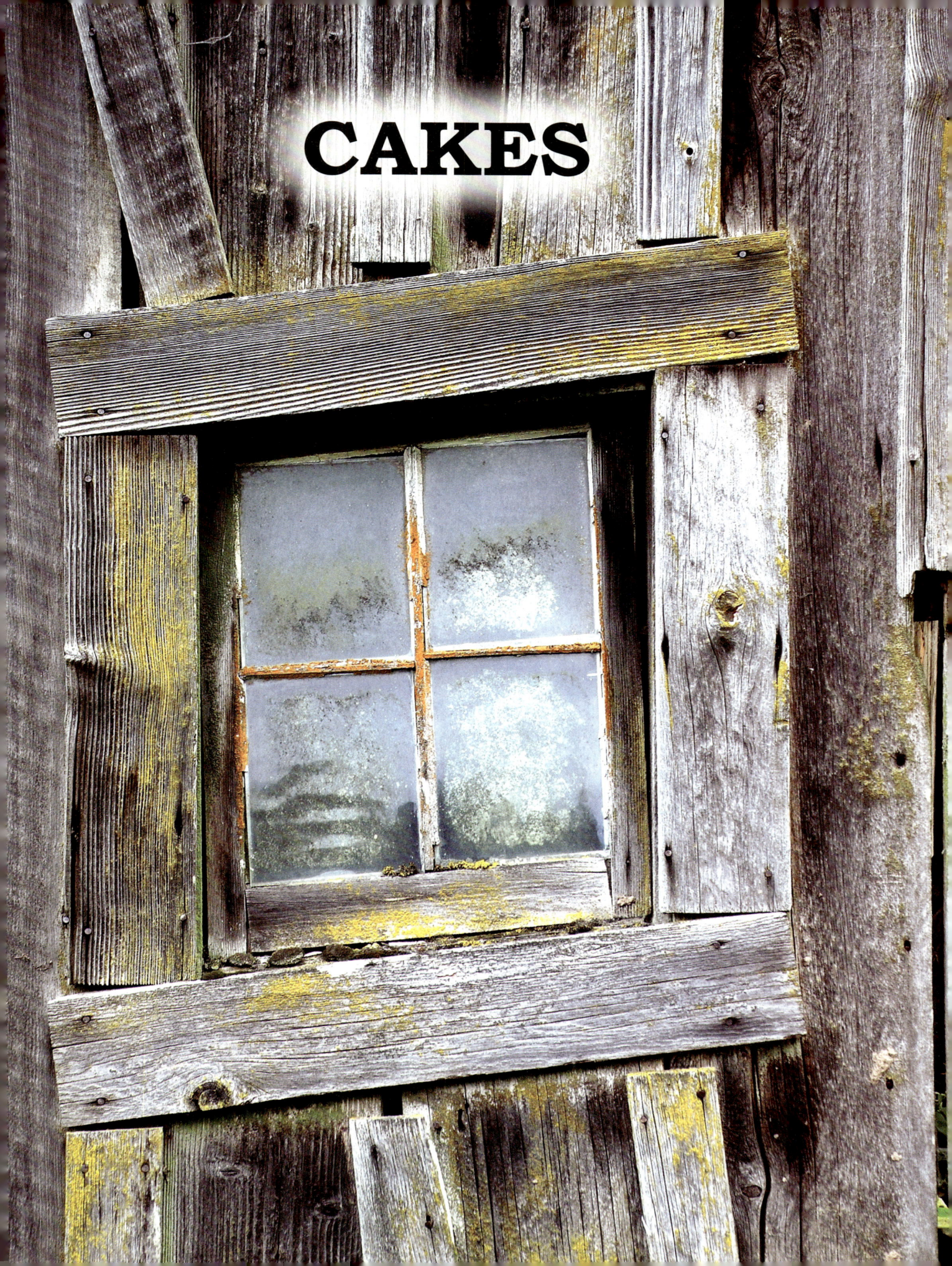

# CAKES

# WACKY CAKE

From Ruthann and Corinne Abernathy. This cake can actually be mixed in the baking pan.

2 cups sugar
3 cups flour
2 tsp. baking soda
1 tsp. baking powder
½ tsp. salt
6 Tbsp. cocoa

1 cup oil
1 egg
1 cup cold water
1 cup strong black coffee
1½ tsp. vinegar
2 tsp. vanilla

Sift together dry ingredients and add liquids; beat until mixed well. Bake at 350° for 45 minutes or until toothpick comes out clean.

# SOUR CREAM POUND CAKE

om Lucille Campbell's country kitchen.

¾ cups sugar

cup butter

eggs

cups flour

tsp. salt

tsp. baking soda

cup dairy sour cream

tsp. lemon extract

tsp. orange extract

tsp. vanilla

mixing bowl cream together sugar and butter until light
d fluffy. Add eggs, one at a time, beating well after each
ddition. Sift together flour, salt, soda; add to creamed
ixture alternately with sour cream, beating after each
ddition. Add extracts and vanilla; beat well. Pour bat-
r into greased and floured 10-inch tube pan. Bake in
50° oven for 1½ hours or until cake tests done. When
ol, frost or sprinkle with powdered sugar, if desired.
ood just plain or with fruit also).

# LILLIE'S CREAM CAKE WITH CARAMEL FROSTING

One of the sweetest recipes from sweet Aunt Lillie Rotschy.

## CAKE:
**Beat 2 eggs well**

Gradually add and continue beating:
1 cup sugar
1 cup whipping cream

Mix in:
½ tsp. salt
2 rounded tsp. baking powder
1½ cups flour

Pour into 9"x 9" pan.
Bake at 350˚ until done.

## FROSTING:
½ cup brown sugar
½ cup white sugar
4 Tbsp. cream
3 Tbsp. butter

Mix all ingredients. Boil 1½ minutes. Cool partially, then beat until creamy and spread over cake.

**This dip can also be used over Lillie's cream cake:**

## CHOCOLATE DIP:
1 cup sugar
2 Tbsp. cornstarch
1 square chocolate
2 cups boiling water
4 Tbsp. butter

# BANANA CAKE

This is definitely a winner!  Recipe from JoAnn Cummings.

Cream together until fluffy:
½ cup shortening
1 ½ cups sugar

Beat in thoroughly:
2 large eggs

Sift together:
2 cups flour
¼ tsp. baking powder
¼ tsp. baking soda
1 tsp. salt

Stir in alternately with:
¼ cup buttermilk
1 cup mashed bananas
1 cup nuts

Beat only enough to mix well. Pour into greased and floured 9" x 13" pan, or two 9" pans. Bake at 350° 25-30 minutes for 9" and 35-40 minutes for 9"x 13".

Whip 1 pint cream for frosting.  Sugar to taste and add 1 tsp. vanilla.  Put some whipped cream on plate before putting down first layer.  This keeps bottom layer moist.  Place sliced bananas and whipped cream on middle layer.  Cover top and sides with rest of whipped cream.  Best to leave in refrigerator for several hours, gets nice and moist.  Before serving put sliced bananas on top of cake.

Heidi remembers this cake from growing up at home in Yacolt: "It was truly the topper to Mom's wholesome cooking!" If you want your folks to say "WOW!", serve this cake for dessert.

# OATMEAL CAKE

Pour:

**1 cup boiling water**

Over:

**1 cup oatmeal**
**1 stick butter (½ cup)**

Let stand 20 minutes covered.

Mix with beater:

**1 cup white sugar**
**1 cup brown sugar**
**2 eggs**
**1 tsp. nutmeg**
**1½ cups flour**
**1 tsp. baking soda**
**1 tsp. cinnamon**
**½ tsp. salt**

Combine and beat well. Bake in a 9"x 13" pan for 30 minutes at 350°.

**ICING:**
**1 stick butter (½ cup)**
**2 cups coconut**
**2 cups chopped nuts**
**¾ cup cream**
**¾ cup sugar**
**1 tsp. vanilla**

Cook over low heat until butter is melted. Spread over cake while both are warm and return to oven for 5 minutes. Then turn on broiler for 2-3 minutes to lightly toast.

Ideals change! Consider the following conclusion of a story written in 1843: "And for the last decade she has become a very fat, comfortable and contented matron."

# SOUR CREAM LEMON POUND CAKE

From Dane Hersey
Moist and flavorful pound cake, like the Starbucks version. Easy to make and freezes extremely well. The taste even improves with age.

2¼ cups sifted flour
⅓ tsp. baking soda
½ cup butter, softened
1½ cups sugar
3 larger eggs, separated, at room temperature
⅔ cup sour cream
1 tsp. vanilla extract
½ cup lemon juice
1 Tbsp. lemon rind, grated fine

Preheat oven to 325°. Butter and flour a bread pan, glass or aluminum. Set aside. Sift together flour and baking soda; set aside. Cream butter and sugar until fluffy, about 3 minutes. Add egg yolks, lemon juice, and beat well. Add ⅓ of the flour mixture and beat to incorporate, then add the sour cream and beat again. Stir in vanilla. Beat egg whites until stiff, then fold into the batter with a over- and –under motion. Pour into the prepared pan. Bake on the center rack of the oven for about 1 hour and 20 minutes or until golden on top and cake tester comes out clean. Let cake cool in the pan on a rack. Drizzle with a glaze (below). It can be stored in an airtight container or frozen.

## GLAZE:

1 cup powdered sugar
1 Tbsp. lemon juice extract

Mix until smooth, glaze consistency. Drizzle over top of cooled pound cake and let harden; refrigerate if needed to harden glaze.

# CARROT CAKE

This recipe is from Joan Reuter. We tasted this moist, delicious cake at Luke's and Debbie's cabin by the Toutle River on the 4th of July. Their neighbors, John and Joan Reuter, brought it over. Joan tells us, "We had this recipe used by the baker who made our wedding cake. We have not come upon a better recipe."

1 cup olive oil
4 eggs
2 cups sugar
2 cups flour
1 cup walnuts, chopped
1 cup raisins
2 tsp. cinnamon
½ tsp. nutmeg
2 tsp. baking powder
2 tsp. baking soda
2 tsp. salt
4 cups grated carrots

Beat the eggs. Add oil and sugar. Mix well. Gradually add the dry ingredients; mix well. Put in 9"x 13" pan; bake at 325° for 55-60 minutes or until toothpick comes out clean. Frost with cream cheese frosting.

## CREAM CHEESE FROSTING:

Combine: ½ cup butter with 8oz. cream cheese, 2 tsp. vanilla and 1 box powdered sugar. Frost the cake when it's cooled. There will be leftover frosting. Joan says, "Put it on soda crackers like my Mommy used to do for us kids."

# ABERNATHY CHOCOLATE CAKE

This recipe originally came from Grandma Anna. It was always made with the frosting listed below. Aunt Pearl was known for making these special cakes. I can just see her loving hands testing the frosting to see if it was ready to beat. Aunt Pearl made me feel extra special and loved in my childhood years.

2 cups brown sugar
½ cup shortening or butter
3 eggs
2 cups flour
1 cup buttermilk
1 heaping tsp. baking soda
2 squares melted chocolate
1 tsp. salt
1 tsp. vanilla
Walnuts (cut up) if desired

Cream brown sugar and shortening/butter together. Add eggs, beating well after each egg. Add flour and salt alternately with buttermilk that has been stirred with soda. Add vanilla and walnuts. Divide equally into 3 round cake pans that have been greased and floured. Bake at 350° for about 25-30 minutes; check with toothpick.

COOKED WHITE FROSTING:
3 cups sugar
1 cup cream, or ½ cream/½ milk

1 Tbsp. cornstarch
3 Tbsp. water
1 tsp. vanilla

Put sugar and cream in saucepan and bring to boil. Add water mixed with cornstarch. Mix and stir to soft ball stage. Cool; beat! Add vanilla and more cream if it gets too thick. If this sugars, just add some more cream and re-cook to soft ball stage. Melt 3 squares of bitter chocolate and pour over this 3 layered cake, letting it drizzle down the sides.

# MOLASSES CAKE
# (THE BEST GINGERBREAD)

My mother-in law Rose gave this to me. It is yummy with whipped cream!

2 eggs
¾ cup brown sugar
¾ cup molasses
¾ cup shortening, melted
1 cup hot water

Sift together:
2½ cups flour
2 tsp. baking soda
1 tsp. ginger
½ tsp. cinnamon
½ tsp. salt
½ tsp. baking powder

Add well beaten eggs to sugar, melted shortening, and molasses. Add dry ingredients. Mix well and lastly add 1 cup hot water. Bake at 350° for 30-35 minutes in greased 9"x 13" pan.

Time is fleeting, years roll by
We are lovers till we die.
We love the earth and love the sun
Love our neighbors everyone.
Romance lingers long as life
Devoted partners, man and wife.

-Chester G. Abernathy

My parents are gone now, but they live close to our hearts in memory. They were indeed partners for life and their beautiful example is a reminder for us all to follow. Mother loved to make the Abernathy cake and Father loved to eat it.

# LARK'S CHOCOLATE CAKE

A wonderful cake, we make it often.  From Lark Hersey.

Mix in bowl:
**2 cups sugar**
**2 cups flour**
**1 tsp. salt**

Mix in saucepan:
**1 cup water**
**2 sticks butter (1 cup)**
**2 heaping Tbsp. cocoa**

Bring to boil and add to dry mixture in bowl; mix well.

Add:
**½ cup buttermilk**
**1 tsp. baking soda**
**1 tsp. vanilla**

Pour in large jelly roll pan and bake at 400° for about 20 minutes.

**FROSTING:**
Melt and bring to boil:
**½ cup butter**
**2 tsp. cocoa**
**⅓ cup milk**
**1 tsp. vanilla**

Add:
**1 box powdered sugar and frost cake while warm.**

Elaine Johnston makes a cake similar to this one.  Her husband got the recipe while he worked at Freightliner, so this is also often called "Freightliner cake."  The variation is:

**A little more cocoa in cake and frosting**
**2 eggs added with buttermilk**
**1 cup coconut and chopped nuts in frosting**

Cake is baked at 350° for 40 minutes in 9"x 13" pan.

# BLACK BOTTOM CAKE

For cream cheese lovers.

Mix together, then set aside:
**1 (8oz.) pkg. cream cheese, softened**
**⅓ cup sugar**
**⅛ tsp salt**
**1 egg**

Sift together:
**1½ cups flour**
**1 cup sugar**
**1 tsp. baking soda**
**½ tsp. salt**
**¼ cup cocoa**

Add to flour mixture:
**⅓ cup oil**
**1 cup cold water**
**1 Tbsp. vinegar**
**1 tsp. vanilla**
**Walnuts, if desired**

Put cake mixture into greased 9"x 13" pan or cupcake papers.  Place spoonful of cream cheese mixture on top of each cupcake or over top of 9"x 13" pan.  Bake at 350° for about 30 minutes.

# SWEET POTATO CAKE
from Maria Tormanen.

1 large can sweet potatoes, drained
1 cup vegetable oil
4 eggs
2 cups sugar
2 cups flour
2 tsp. baking powder
1 tsp. salt
1 Tbsp. cinnamon
1 tsp. nutmeg
2 tsp. vanilla
1 cup macadamia nuts, chopped

Preheat oven to 325°. Butter and flour 2 round cake pans. Beat eggs and sugar for 5 minutes. Puree potatoes in blender. Add oil and potatoes to eggs. Sift together dry ingredients. Mix into wet ingredients. Add vanilla and fold in nuts. Bake 40-45 minutes.

## FROSTING:
1 lb. white chocolate
2 cups cream

Boil 1 cup cream. Chop chocolate and stir in pan until melted. Chill. Whip remaining cream and fold into chocolate mixture. Maria says, "makes enough to frost a layer cake, but I usually do it a layer at a time because it's so rich."

# UPSIDE-DOWN BERRY CORN MEAL CAKE
Great for the summertime.

2 - 2½ cups fresh blueberries, raspberries, and/or blackberries
1⅓ cups all-purpose flour
½ cup yellow corn meal
2 tsp. baking powder
¼ tsp. salt
2 eggs, lightly beaten
½ cup sugar
⅔ cup milk
⅓ cup oil

Arrange 1½ cups of berries on the bottom of a round cake pan that has been well greased. Set aside. Sift together dry ingredients. Beat together eggs, sugar, milk, and oil. Add egg mixture to sifted dry ingredients. Stir well. Pour into pan over berries; spread evenly. Bake at 350° for 40 minutes or until toothpick comes clean. Cool cake in pan for 5 minutes; run knife around edges; then invert. Top with remaining berries. It can be frosted with a light glaze.

# APPLE DAPPLE CAKE

This recipe is from Kristi Kysar. She says, "This recipe originated from Lillian Lehtola. I remember mom baking this cake when I was young, it was my favorite."

Cream together:
**3 eggs**
**2 cups sugar**
**1 cup oil**

Sift together:
**3 cups flour**
**1 tsp. cinnamon**
**1 tsp. baking soda**
**1 tsp. salt**

Mix egg and flour mixture together.
Add:
**1 cup coconut**
**1 cup nuts, chopped**
**3 cups apples, diced**
**2 tsp. vanilla**

Batter of cake is stiff. Bake at 350° for 45-60 minutes.

**ICING:**
**1 cup brown sugar**
**½ cup butter**
**¼ cup milk**

Boil together for 3 minutes. Put icing on cake right after baking when cake is hot. After pouring icing on cake, use a meat fork, piercing cake all over the top so icing will seep in.

# PIES & PASTRIES

## WILD BERRY BUCKLE

Mix like pie crust. This is easy and very good!

2½ cups flour
1 Tbsp. sugar
1 tsp. salt
1 cup shortening
1 egg; add enough milk to make
⅔ cup

Filling for each buckle:
2 cups berries
½ cup sugar
1 Tbsp. butter

This should make 3 round pans. Divide dough. Roll out 3 buckles, fitting dough in a 9" pie pan; allow a 2" overhang. Do one buckle at a time. Add berries to crust. Sprinkle with sugar. Dot with butter. Fold edges over berries, leave the center open. Bake for 35-45 minutes at 350˚.

## THE BERRY NICE SURPRISE

...ose Anna Gillette just celebrated her 101st birthday on June 5th, 2007. The good fortune of having ...r in my life through every stage—childhood, young adult, parenthood, and now a grandmother ...yself—naturally has made a patchwork of colorful experiences and lessons learned. One of my ...st surprises took place when I was a young mother. I walked into Grandma Rosie's old farmhouse ...tchen and smelled mouth-watering huckleberry pie. The vintage Monarch cook stove was radiating ...eat and she was standing beside it with a potholder in her hand, an apron over her dress, and a ...eet smile on her face.

...Why, Heidi, you are here today!"

...es, Grandma Rosie, and a fine day it is. You sure look happy. I bet it's on account of the ...onderful berry pie you're baking."

...ell, no, it isn't a pie....(chuckle, chuckle)..."

...eally, are you serious, Grandma? I've smelled a lot of pies baking before and that has to be berry ...e. Not just berry, but real, real, good berry. What is it, huckleberry?"

...hhh, not exactly...."

... give up if it's not some kind of berry pie. Whatever could make my mouth water like pie and not ... pie?"

... will show you... see it is bear fat that I'm rendering down for your father. He shot a bear last week ...d would like to have it to grease his boots. This bear has been eating huckleberries all summer ...ng, so his fat smells like the whole pie. You know it does make good pastry."

-Heidi Esteb

THE POULTRY PALACE

"I rule the roost," crowed the Rooster.
"I rule the rooster," clucked the Hen.

# BANANA PUDDING PIE

My mother was from the South and this recipe came with her.

**1 box vanilla wafer cookies**
**½ cup butter, melted**
**3 medium bananas, sliced**
**Vanilla cream pudding**
**4 egg whites**
**½ cup sugar**

You can make it two ways. You can line a 9" pie plate with the wafers on the bottom and sides of pie plate, OR crush ¾ of the box of cookies until coarsely crushed; this should be a little over 2 cups of crumbs. Mix crumbs with butter. Firmly press crumbs on the bottom and up sides of pie plate. Bake at 350° for about 10 minutes. Remove from oven; let cool. Arrange banana slices over bottom of crust. Pour ½ of prepared vanilla pudding over bananas. Top with more wafers and bananas and pour the rest of pudding on top. Beat egg whites, gradually adding sugar until stiff peaks form and sugar is dissolved. Spread meringue evenly over hot filling; seal edges. Bake for 12 minutes or until golden brown. Remove from oven, allow to cool. You can sprinkle with a few cookie crumbs. Chill.

# VANILLA CREAM PIE

From Patience Rose, a good cream pie.

**2 cups milk**
**2 cups Half & Half**
**2 Tbsp. cornstarch**
**½ tsp. salt**
**6 Tbsp. flour**
**1 cup sugar**
**4 egg yolks**
**2 tsp. vanilla**

Scald milk and cream in double boiler. Combine flour, cornstarch, sugar, and salt. Mix together thoroughly. Add to scalded milk and cook 15 minutes, stirring constantly. Pour slowly over slightly beaten egg yolks and return to double boiler. Cook 1 minute. Cool and add vanilla. Pour into pie shell and top with meringue.

# APPLES, APPLES, APPLES

The glorious smell of applesauce, pies, cobblers, and apple butter often emerged from the old cook stove. That old stove was the heart of country living when you didn't have electricity. It gave aromas that made a child's heart swell with love and anticipation. I still remember the apple trees swaying in the wind, weighted down with their precious fruit. Yellow Transparent apples were so yummy! They are hard to come by nowadays.

–Linda Kysar

# APPLE PIE

America's favorite! Apple pie without the cheese is like a kiss without the squeeze! Make pie crust for two-crust pie. Roll out one-half of dough and line 9" pie pan.

Mix together:
**6-8 cups tart apples**
**1-1½ cups sugar**
**⅓ cup flour**
**About 1 tsp. cinnamon**
**Pinch of salt**
**Butter**

Pour all ingredients into pie shell except butter. Dot with butter. Cover with top crust which has slits or a design cut into it. Seal and flute. Bake until crust is nicely browned and apples are done (test with a fork). Bake at 375° for about 50 minutes. Oh, that wonderful aroma that fills my country kitchen! Serve warm or cold.

I always cover the fluted crust edges with foil; this keeps the edges from browning too fast.

# DON'T MESS UP THE OVEN APPLE PIE

From Kay Dalke. Wonderful!

**6-8 Yellow Transparent apples or other tart apples**
**1 cup sugar**
**¼ cup (less if not too juicy) flour**
**¼ tsp. cinnamon**
**Butter**

Mix all ingredients together except butter, and heat in microwave, stirring gently 2-3 times until almost cooked through. Put in prepared pie crust, dot with butter, and cover with top crust. Prick top with fork and sprinkle sugar and cinnamon mixture on top. Bake at 350° until crust is brown and filling bubbles through the crust. You can make the same pie using 4-6 cups of berries.

# GAIL'S RHUBARB PIE

Gail Schmeusser says that this pie looks so pretty with the red coloring. She and Roger put up lots of rhubarb every spring.

3 cups rhubarb, finely chopped
1 cup sugar
1 Tbsp. flour per cup rhubarb
Dash of red food coloring
1 cup pineapple, diced small
Butter

This is for a small pie; you can add additional rhubarb and flour accordingly. Mix all together except butter; pour into unbaked pie crust, dot with real butter and cover with pie crust of choice. Cut vents on top and sprinkle with sugar; bake at 400° for 45 minutes. Cover edge of crust with aluminum foil during baking.

# LILLIE'S CARAMEL PIE

Cousin Shelley Heidegger says, "I can remember taking this to a pie social in the old upstairs kitchen of Yacolt School. The neighbor boy bid it up so high because he knew how good it was. I would have liked to think that it was because he wanted to eat with me, but I think he knew Mom (Lillie Rotschy) had made the pie." This is a very old family recipe.

Brown
**2 cups white sugar** in heavy skillet until light brown. Watch so that it doesn't burn.

Add
**2 cups hot water** and let cook until sugar is melted. Then cool.

Combine
**4 egg yolks** (save whites for meringue)
**6½ tsp. flour and 2 cups milk.**

Pour into cooled sugar mixture and cook until thick, stirring constantly.

Mix a little of the milk with the flour so it doesn't lump.

Remove from heat and add
**4 Tbsp. butter and a pinch of salt.**

Pour into baked pie shell, cover with meringue and bake at 375° for 10-12 minutes until meringue is golden brown.

# COCONUT CREAM PIE

Guaranteed to please!

**2 cups milk**
**2 cups Half & Half**
**2 Tbsp. cornstarch**
**6 Tbsp. flour**
**1 cup sugar**
**1 egg and 3 egg yolks**
**2 tsp. vanilla**
**2 Tbsp. butter**
**2 cups coconut**

Heat milk and cream. (I do this in the microwave.) Mix flour, corn starch, and sugar together. Whisk into hot milk. Put back into microwave, stirring every 2 minutes, until it has boiled. Beat eggs until lemon colored. Slowly add hot mixture to eggs, this will keep them from cooking too fast. Cook for 1 minute longer. Add butter, vanilla, and coconut. Pour into cooled, baked crust. Serve with whipped cream.

# CHOCOLATE PIE

So quick and easy!

I use 1 box of JELL-O Cook and Serve Pudding. I add 2 cups Half & Half with 1 cup milk. I also add 2 Hershey's chocolate bars and 2 Tbsp. butter after filling has boiled. Everyone loves this pie. Top with whipped cream.

# FRESH MARION BERRY PIE

I usually cover crimped edges with foil while baking.

Make pie crust for two crust pie.

**FILLING:**
**4-5 cups fresh berries**
**1 cup sugar**
**1/3 cup flour**
**Butter**

Line pan with crust. Pour filling into crust, except butter. Dot with butter and top with top crust which has slits in it. Cover edge with aluminum foil; bake at 400° for 45 minutes. Bake until crust is nicely browned and juice begins to bubble through slits.

* Refer to page 131—the quick way to make this pie.

# SWEDISH CREAM

Elaine Sarkinen says, "This must go in your book." She was served this over fresh fruit at Logan and Alyssa Kysar's home.

**1 cup sour cream**
**1/2 cup sugar**
**1/2 cup plain yogurt**
**1 Tbsp. vanilla**
**3 Tbsp. orange juice**
   **(optional)**
**2 cups whipping cream**

Combine sour cream, sugar, yogurt, vanilla, and orange juice in bowl. Scald whipping cream over medium heat; when bubbles form around edge of pan, remove from heat and mix with other ingredients. Refrigerate for several hours. Note: Half & Half may be substituted for whipping cream. This pourable cream topping is delectable over fresh fruit and berry desserts.

# SOUTHERN PECAN PIE

Rekindles memories of going home to grandma's! From my mother's homeland, North Carolina.

**1/2 cup butter**
**1 cup sugar**
**1 cup dark or light corn syrup**
**2 cups pecans**
**4 eggs, beaten**
**1 tsp. vanilla**
**1/4 tsp. salt**

Cream butter and sugar. Add eggs and rest of ingredients. Pour into pie shell. Bake until done, about 45 minutes to 1 hour at 325°.

Live everyday for the lives
f those who have fallen."

- Corporal Fox, Spenser USMC
  Served two tours in Iraq
  Currently stationed at 29 Palms, California
  September 4th, 2007
4TH YEAR SERVING AMERICA

Oh, how we farm children dreamed of owning a bicycle. A real bicycle! Finally, we got one bike to share and we learned to ride it. The scrapes and skinned up knees were plentiful. Our cousins lived close by, and they also got a bike to share. It felt like we owned the world, when our turn came, racing along with another bicycle beside us. Those thrills cannot be duplicated today!

# PEACH COBBLER

We got this recipe from an old Amish cookbook years ago. When you find a recipe that turns out every time and is easy to make, you like to share it. Here it is.

1 Tbsp. cornstarch
¼ cup brown sugar
½ cup cold water
4-5 fresh peaches, sliced
1 Tbsp. butter

**COBBLER CRUST**
1 cup flour
½ cup sugar
1½ tsp. baking powder
½ tsp. salt
½ cup milk
¼ cup butter, melted

Mix first three ingredients with fruit. Cook and stir until thick. Add butter. Pour into 9"x13" pan. Sift dry ingredients; add milk and melted butter. Beat until smooth. Spread over fruit. Sprinkle with cinnamon and sugar. Bake at 350° for 30-40 minutes. Serve warm with ice cream or Half & Half. We usually double this recipe and we use any fresh fruit. If you double this recipe, bake in large 15"x10" Pyrex glass pan.

# LEMON-CRUSTED BLUEBERRY PIE

This recipe is from Lucille Campbell.

Mix together:
⅓ cup boiling water
⅔ cup shortening
1 tsp. salt

Add:
½ tsp. lemon peel
2 cups flour

**FILLING:**
4 cups blueberries, fresh or frozen
1 cup sugar
3 Tbsp. flour
½ tsp. grated lemon peel
Dash of salt
1 Tbsp. butter

Mix only until holds together. Divide in half and roll each crust between 2 sheets of waxed paper. Remove one sheet of paper and lay crust over pan and then remove other sheet. Fill with blueberry filling, except butter.

Sprinkle 1-2 tsp. lemon juice over top of filling and dot with 1 Tbsp. butter. Add top crust and bake in 400° oven for 15 minutes, then at 350° for an additional 25-30 minutes.

# FRAN'S LEMON MERINGUE PIE

I got this recipe from Selma Stephenson. She brought this pie and delicious brown bread with raisins to our home many years ago.

Mix in a saucepan:
**1½ cups sugar**
**⅓ cup cornstarch**
**1½ cups water**
**3 egg yolks**
**3 Tbsp. butter**
**½ cup fresh lemon juice**
**Grated lemon rind**

Cook first 3 ingredients slowly over medium heat, stirring constantly, until mixture thickens and boils. Boil 1 minute. Slowly stir at least half the hot mixture into 3 egg yolks, slightly beaten. Then blend into hot mixture in saucepan. Boil 1 minute longer, stirring constantly. Remove from heat and blend in 3 Tbsp. butter and ½ cup fresh lemon juice, with a little grated lemon rind. Fold in ¼ of beaten meringue into filling and top with remaining meringue.

# KEY LIME PIE

From Rochelle Bellika. Rochelle brings her pies everywhere she goes!

**1- 9" graham cracker crust, cooked and cooled**
**½ cup key lime juice**
**1 cup sweetened condensed milk**
**Green food coloring**
**8oz. carton Cool Whip**

Mix the key lime juice with the sweetened condensed milk. Add 1-2 drops green food coloring. Stir in the Cool Whip and pour into crust. Refrigerate for 4 hours or longer. Garnish with sliced limes or flowers on top of pie.

138

# BE-BOP RHUBARB PIE

A western treat from Cheryl Crume.

**No roll Pastry:**
1½ cups flour
1 tsp. salt
1 Tbsp. sugar
½ tsp. oil
2 Tbsp. 2% milk

Mix flour, salt, and sugar. Pour in oil and milk. Mix with fork and spread into deep dish pie pan.

**FILLING:**
6-7 cups rhubarb, cut up
2 cups sugar
6 Tbsp. flour
1 Tbsp. butter, cut up

Combine rhubarb, sugar, and flour. Dot with butter.

**TOPPING:**
¼ cup butter, cut into pieces
¼ cup sugar
½ cup flour
2 Tbsp. sliced almonds

Mix butter, sugar, flour, and almonds with pastry blender. Sprinkle over filling. Bake at 350° for 1 hour.

# NEVER FAIL PIE CRUST

Cut shortening into flour and salt until mixture is the size of small peas. Add water, vinegar, and beaten egg.

**3 cups flour**
**1 tsp. salt**
**1½ cups shortening**
**1 beaten egg**
**1 Tbsp. vinegar**
**4 Tbsp. water**

# NEVER FAIL MERINGUE

A beautiful meringue.

Combine in small sauce pan:
**2 Tbsp. sugar**
**1 Tbsp. cornstarch**

Add:
**½ cup water**

Cook over medium heat, stirring constantly, until mixture is thick and clear. Cool.

Beat until soft mounds form:
**3 egg whites**
**⅛ tsp. salt**
**½ tsp. vanilla**

Add:
**6 Tbsp. sugar,** gradually, beating well after each addition.

Add:
Cornstarch mixture. Beat until meringue stands in stiff peaks. Bake at 350° for 12-15 minutes.

# PIE CRUST FROM OLD GRANGE COOKBOOK

From Kay Dalke. This recipe is fantastic!

**2 cups flour**
**1 cup shortening**
**1 tsp. salt**

Mix together and add:
**⅓ cup milk mixed with 1 tsp. vinegar**

Mix together and roll out. Don't be afraid to add flour to the top and bread-board to roll out as it is pretty hard to make this pie crust tough.

# COOKIES & BARS

# OATMEAL COOKIES

A moist oatmeal cookie from Karen McDaniels.

1¼ cups flour
1 tsp. baking soda
1 cup butter
¾ cup white sugar
¾ cup brown sugar
1 pkg. instant vanilla pudding
2 eggs
3½ cups oatmeal
1 cup raisins

Cream butter, sugars, and eggs; add dry ingredients. Drop on greased baking sheet and bake at 375° for 10-12 minutes. If desired, add chocolate chips, nuts, etc.

# MARIA'S CHOCOLATE CHIP COOKIES
From Corinne Abernathy.

1 cup brown sugar
¼ cup sugar
1 cup butter
2 eggs
1 tsp. vanilla
3 cups flour
1 tsp. salt
1 tsp. baking soda
1½ cups chocolate chips

Mix sugars and butter until well combined. Stir in eggs one at a time; add vanilla. In another bowl, combine flour, salt, and baking soda. Add to butter mixture with chocolate chips. Drop by spoonfuls. Bake at 350° for 10-12 minutes.

"It is because of those at home that I serve. I'm not doing this just for me. Knowing people are grateful is very appreciated. Honestly, you do not have enough room in this book to write what I feel about America!"

**-AT2 Beatty, Phillip U.S. Navy**
Naval Air crewman, Goldwings/Sea Hawk, Air warfare qualified, Naval Rescue swimmer
Served 2 tours in Iraq–June 04 - May 2007
Currently stationed at Blioxi, MS Sept 11th, 2007

*6TH YEAR SERVING AMERICA*

# THE OLD WOOD STACK

The almanac said a bad winter was on its way
The weather was getting cold, the wind began to blow;
But tucked away in the shed all nice and dry
Was promised warmth, stacked in a row.

This firewood was not easy to come by
It took time to be cut, chopped, and stacked;
It calloused many a hand, dulled the old saw
And out of the woods, it had to be packed.

But all the hard work and sawdust in the boots
Is soon forgotten, when the weather gets cold;
You can sit by the crackling fire
And listen to old stories be told.

And all and all, we need heat in the winter
It's the firewood that keeps us warm;
So make sure you've got some dry wood
When in blows the first winter storm.
                    -Jude Homola

# BUTTER COOKIES

JoAnn makes dozens of these buttery cookies on Valentine's Day for everyone.

1 cup butter, softened
½ cup sugar
1 egg
3 tsp. flavoring of choice
  (vanilla, lemon, almond, etc.)
3 cups sifted flour
½ tsp. baking powder

Cream butter, sugar, and egg; stir in flavoring. Sift together flour and baking powder and add to creamed mixture. Chill dough. Roll very thin, cut into desired shapes. Place on ungreased baking sheet. Bake at 400° for 7-9 minutes.

BUTTER ICING:
3 cups powdered sugar
½ cup melted butter
2 Tbsp. milk
1 tsp. vanilla
⅛ tsp. salt

Sift sugar, combine with melted butter, vanilla, salt, milk. Beat until creamy.

# BANANA OATMEAL COOKIES

This recipe is from Louise Fraiser.

**1½ cups flour**
**1 cup sugar**
**½ tsp. baking soda**
**1 tsp. salt**
**¼ tsp. nutmeg**
**¾ tsp. cinnamon**
**¾ cup shortening**
**1 egg, well beaten**
**1 cup mashed bananas**
**1¾ cups quick-cooking oatmeal**
**½ cup chopped walnuts**

Sift together dry ingredients. Cut in shortening. Add egg, bananas, rolled oats, and nuts. Drop by teaspoonfuls onto ungreased cookie sheet. Bake at 375° about 15 minutes. Makes 3 dozen cookies.

# MOLASSES OAT COOKIES WITH WHITE CHOCOLATE

From daughter Heather. Great with coffee!

Mix together well:
**1 cup butter, softened**
**2 cups brown sugar**
**½ cup white sugar**
**¾ cup molasses**
**4 eggs**

ADD:
**4 cups flour**
**1 tsp. baking soda**
**1 tsp. baking powder**
**1 tsp. salt**

ADD and mix well:
**4 cups oats**
**1 bag white chocolate chips**

Place good sized mounds of dough (as big as an ice cream scoop) on greased cookie sheet. Bake at 375° for 13-15 minutes until golden.

# SOFT MOLASSES COOKIES

The smell from these ginger cookies radiates through the kitchen.

1½ cups shortening
¼ cup butter
2 cups brown sugar
½ cup molasses
2 eggs
4½ cups flour
4 tsp. baking soda
1 tsp. ginger
1 tsp. cinnamon
½ tsp. salt

Cream together shortening and butter with sugar, molasses, and eggs until fluffy. Sift together dry ingredients, stir into sugar mixture. Add about ½ cup hot water. Drop by rounded spoonfuls onto baking sheet. Bake at 375° for 12 minutes. Frost with a butter frosting.

# GRANDMA LIZZIE'S MOLASSES COOKIES

I am the third generation to make these wonderful cookies. You cannot beat them.

1 cup sugar
1 cup butter
1 cup molasses
1 egg
1 Tbsp. vinegar
1 tsp. ginger
1 tsp. baking soda
A little hot water
4 cups flour

Mix all ingredients together and chill. Roll out to your own desired thickness and cut to shapes for the occasion. Bake at 375° for 7-10 minutes. These cookies can be frosted.

# OATMEAL CRISPIES

Recipe from daughter-in-law, Kristy Gillette. She got the recipe from her Grandma Kaski.

CREAM:
**1 cup shortening**
**2 cups brown sugar**

ADD:
**2 eggs, beaten well**
**1 tsp. vinegar**

ADD:
**1½ cups flour**
**½ tsp. salt**
**1 tsp. cinnamon**
**2 tsp. baking powder**

ADD:
**2 cups oatmeal**
**½ cup chopped raisins**
**½ cup nutmeats**

Bake at 375° for about 10 minutes.

# GINGERSNAPS

From Corinne Abernathy.

¾ cup shortening
1 cup sugar
¼ cup molasses
1 egg
2½ cups flour

2 tsp. baking soda
½ tsp. salt
1 tsp. ginger
1 tsp. cinnamon
½ tsp. cloves

Cream together the first 2 ingredients until fluffy; stir in molasses and egg. Add dry sifted ingredients. Form balls and roll in the sugar. Bake at 375° for 10 minutes.

# BEST NO-BAKE COOKIES

This recipe is a winner. My girls have been making this recipe for years.

Bring to a good boil:

**2 cups sugar**
**½ cup butter**
**¼ cup cocoa**
**½ cup milk**.

Remove from heat and add:

**¼ cup peanut butter**
**1 tsp. vanilla**
**3 cups rolled oats**
**1 cup nuts chopped**
**1 cup coconut**

Stir until mixture thickens and drop spoonfuls onto wax paper.

# SUPER DUPER CHOCOLATE COOKIES

My family loves these cookies; the recipe is from Raydene McDaniels.

**½ cup shortening**
**4 squares unsweetened chocolate**
**2 cups sugar**
**2 tsp. vanilla**
**4 eggs, unbeaten**
**2 cups flour**
**2 tsp. baking powder**
**⅛ tsp. salt**
**½ cup chopped nuts**

**Confectioners sugar**

Melt shortening and chocolate; add sugar and vanilla; mix well. Add eggs, one at a time, beating after each. Sift flour, baking powder, and salt; add to chocolate mixture with nuts; mix well. Chill dough several hours. Form into small balls; roll in confectioner's sugar. Bake at 350° for 12-15 minutes. Makes 6 dozen.

# EREAL COOKIES

om my daughter-in-law, Kristy. She says, "I got this
cipe from my grandma, Wilma Kaski, and her family
s enjoyed them when they were growing up."

cup sugar
cup brown sugar
cup shortening
eggs
cups flour
cups cornflakes
cups oatmeal
tsp. baking powder
tsp. baking soda
tsp. vanilla
 tsp. salt
cup nuts
conut (optional)

eam sugar and shorten-
g; add eggs and vanilla.
ork in dry ingredients and
ake small walnut sized
lls. Bake at 375° for about
minutes.

# STIR-N-DROP SUGAR COOKIES

We've been making these cookies for years!

2 eggs
⅔ cup oil
1 tsp. vanilla
1 cup sugar
2 cups flour
2 tsp. baking powder
½ tsp. salt

Mix eggs, oil, and vanilla thoroughly. Add sugar and mix until thick. Blend in dry ingredients. Drop by teaspoonfuls on
lightly greased cookie sheet and
flatten with greased bottom of
glass that has been dipped in
sugar. I usually place a nut in
the center of each cookie. Bake
8 minutes at 375°.

## M&M COOKIES

Children love these pretty cookies. I got th[e] recipe years ago from Donna Nelson.

1 cup shortening
1 cup brown sugar
½ cup sugar
2 tsp. vanilla
2 eggs
2¼ cups flour
1 tsp. baking soda
1 tsp. salt
1½ cups m&ms

Cream together shortening, sugars, egg[s] and vanilla; mix well. Add dry ingred[i]ents; mix. Fold in ½ cup m&ms. Drop [by] teaspoonfuls onto greased cookie she[et]. Decorate tops of cookies with remaini[ng] m&ms. Bake at 350° for 12 minutes.

## MONSTER COOKIES

These cookies are fun for children or adults. Lori says, "You feel extra special when one of these is handed to you." You are not confused: there is no flour in this recipe!

9 cups oatmeal
3 cups peanut butter
1 cup butter
2 cups brown sugar
2 cups white sugar

6 eggs
1½ tsp. corn syrup
4 tsp. baking soda
2 tsp. vanilla
1 pkg. mini or regular m&ms.

Mix all ingredients well; spoon out large portioned spoonfuls onto cookie sheet. Bake at 350° for approx. 14 minutes. Makes 4 sheets of 10 cookies each.

# CHOCOLATE CHIP OATMEAL COOKIES

Wonderful cookies from Ruby Kysar.

1¼ cup soft butter
¾ cup brown sugar
½ cup white sugar
1 tsp. vanilla
1 egg

Mix together and add:
1½ cups flour
1 tsp. baking soda
1 tsp. salt
1 tsp. cinnamon (optional)
3 cups old fashioned oatmeal
1-2 cups chocolate chips

Drop by teaspoonfuls on cookie sheet. Do not overbake. Bake at 375° for 12-15 minutes.

# ULTIMATE BAR COOKIES

From Maria Tormanen. Very good!

2 cups flour
½ cup brown sugar
½ cup butter
1 cup macadamia nuts, chopped
6oz. white chocolate, chopped
1 cup milk chocolate chips
¾ cup butter
½ cup brown sugar

**CRUST:**
Beat flour, sugar, and butter until mixture forms fine crumbs. Pat onto bottom of ungreased 9"x 13" pan. Bake at 350° for 15 minutes.

**TOPPING:**
Sprinkle nuts, white chocolate, and chocolate chips on hot crust. When melted, spread. Heat the ¾ cup butter and ½ cup brown sugar in a pan over medium heat until bubbly. Cook, stirring 1 minute more. Pour evenly over crust. Bake at 350° for 12-15 minutes or until just bubbly around edges. Cool.
Can be doubled and put into jelly-roll pan.

# PECAN SANDIES

From Imogene Woodside.

1 cup butter
1 tsp. vanilla
½ cup sugar
2 cups flour
1 cup pecans, finely
    chopped

Cream butter and sugar, stir in vanilla. Add flour. Mixed until blended. Stir in pecans, mixing well. Chill 30 minutes. Roll into one inch balls. Bake at 350 for 15-18 minutes. Yields 3 dozen.

# LEMON BARS

This is Bob Peck's specialty.

2 cups flour
½ cup sugar
1 cup butter

Mix together; press in 9"x 13" pan; bake at 350° for 15 minutes.

2 cups sugar
4 eggs
¼ cup flour
6 Tbsp. lemon juice

Pour on top of crust; bake 15 minutes longer at 350°. This is a favorite any time—everywhere.

# BROWNIES

I got this recipe from my cousin, Shelley Heidegger, years ago. She said, "The secret to good brownies is beating the eggs and sugar until the sugar is dissolved."

Melt:
**⅔ cup shortening**
**4 squares chocolate**

Beat:
**4 eggs** (beat well)
**2 cups sugar**
**1½ cups flour**
**½ tsp. salt**

Add:
Chocolate and shortening
**1 cup nuts**
**1 tsp. baking powder**
**2 tsp. vanilla**
**1 cup nuts, chopped**

Pour into a 9"x 13" pan and bake at 325° for 25-30 minutes.

154

# FUDGY BROWNIES

When our daughter-in-law, Debbie, wanted me to make brownies for her and Luke's wedding from this recipe, I immediately noticed that there was no leavening. "Oh, dear," I thought. "I know these won't turn out." I guess one is never too old to learn. Please try them. They are better than good.

½ cup butter
2 (1oz.) squares unsweetened chocolate
1 cup sugar
2 eggs
1 tsp. vanilla
½ cup flour
¼ tsp. salt
½ cup chopped walnuts

Heat butter and chocolate in 2-quart sauce pan over low heat until melted; remove from heat. Mix in sugar, eggs, and vanilla. Stir in rest of ingredients. Spread in greased 9"x9"x2" pan. Bake at 350° for 20-25 minutes, or until brownies begin to pull away from sides of pan. Cool and cut into 1-inch squares. (Recipe may be doubled and baked in 9"x13" pan.)

# QUICK BROWNIE FROSTING

A wonderful topping for brownies!

1 cup packed sugar
3 Tbsp. butter
¼ cup cream
1 square unsweetened chocolate
½ tsp. vanilla

Mix sugar, butter, cream, and chocolate in a heavy pan. Boil over medium heat for 2 minutes, stirring constantly. Remove from heat and add vanilla. Beat without cooling until thick enough to spread. Delicious!

# SUGAR CRESCENTS

My mother made these when I was a child. Such warm memories.

½ cup butter
3 Tbsp. powdered sugar
1 cup flour
1 cup nuts, finely chopped

Mix together and shape into half moon or crescent shape. Bake at 350° for 10-15 minutes. When cool roll in powdered sugar.

"I will bleed on the flag to keep the stripes red."

-Corporal Kelly, Adam USMC
Served two tours in Iraq
Currently stationed at 29 Palms, California
September 4th, 2007

4TH YEAR SERVING AMERICA

## OLD FASHIONED FRIED PIES

We used to make these all the time. A good, old-time American pie.

2 cups dried peaches, apples
  or apricots, chopped
½ cup of sugar
2 Tbsp. butter, melted
2 cups flour
1 tsp. salt
½ cup shortening
⅔-1 cup ice water

Put fruit in a sauce pan; cover with water. Boil and cook for about 30 minutes, adding water to cover fruit. Drain well. Stir in sugar and melted butter. Set aside. Place flour over salt and shortening in a bowl. Use pastry blender until mixture is crumbly. Sprinkle in water, a little at a time until well moistened. Divide dough into thirds. Roll each portion to ⅛" thickness on a lightly floured surface. Cut into 4½" rounds. Place 1 heaping tsp. of fruit filling in each pastry circle. Moisten edges with water. Fold pastry over filling, pressing edges together to seal. Crimp edges with a fork dipped in flour. Pierce tops with fork. Fry in hot vegetable oil for 3-4 minutes or until golden brown, turning once. Drain on paper towels. Sprinkle with sugar or powdered sugar.

# PEANUT BUTTER FINGERS

That good peanut butter taste!
We make these often.

Cream:
**½ cup butter**
**½ cup sugar**
**½ cup brown sugar**

Blend in:
**1 unbeaten egg**
**⅓ cup peanut butter**
**½ tsp. baking soda**
**¼ tsp. salt**
**½ tsp. vanilla**

Stir in:
**1 cup flour**
**1 cup rolled oats**

Bake at 350° for 20-25 minutes.
Remove from oven and sprinkle with
**1 (6oz.) pkg. chocolate chips.**

Spread chocolate evenly.
Mix:
**½ cup powdered sugar**
**¼ cup peanut butter**
**2-4 Tbsp. evaporated milk**

Drizzle this mixture over chocolate

# RHUBARB DREAM BARS

This recipe comes from Michigan. My sister-in-law Ruthann
brought this recipe along with many other good ones.

Mix well and put into 9"x13" pan:
**1¾ cups flour**
**1 cup butter**
**⅔ cup powdered sugar**

Bake 15 minutes at 350°.
Beat well:
**3 eggs**

Add:
**1¾ cups sugar**
**½ cup flour**
**1 tsp. salt**
**5 cups rhubarb, cut small**

Blend well and spoon onto crust. Bake
at 350° for 40-45 minutes.

## CHOCOLATE CHIP BARS

Yvonne Heidegger gave me this recipe when she lived in Yacolt years ago. An easy way to make chocolate chip cookies.

½ cup butter
¼ cup plus 2 Tbsp. sugar
¼ cup plus 2 Tbsp. brown
   sugar
½ tsp. vanilla
1 egg

1 cup flour
½ tsp. salt
½ tsp. baking soda
½ cup nuts
1 cup chocolate chips

Combine all ingredients; pour into a lightly greased 9" x 13" pan. Bake at 350° for 3-4 minutes, remove from oven and swirl batter tenderly to attain marbled look. Return to oven for 10 minutes. Cut into squares and cool.

# MARLIS' LEMON BARS

From Marlis Peters. For the picture, I used raspberry jam.

½ cup butter
2 cups white chocolate chips
2 large eggs
½ cup sugar
1 cup flour
½ tsp. salt
½ tsp. lemon extract
¼ cup toasted almonds, sliced
¾ cup canned lemon
  pie filling

Preheat oven to 325°. Butter and sugar a 9" x 13" pan. Melt butter in medium, microwaveable bowl, then stir. Add 1 cup white chocolate chips; let stand. Beat eggs until foamy; add sugar, butter, chocolate mixture, flour, salt and lemon extract. Spread ½ of the batter into pan. Bake for 15 minutes. Remove from oven. Pour lemon filling over warm crust. Add 1 cup of white chocolate chips to remaining batter. Then drop spoonfuls of batter over lemon pie filling. Put almonds on top of batter. Bake for 23 minutes or until brown. Cool and cut into bars.

You can use other fillings such as strawberry, blackberry, raspberry, and apricot jam.

"He is doing just what he always has wanted to do. After coming over from Norway as a 9 year old boy and learning American culture, Michael chose to grow up and be a U.S. soldier. He doesn't want to be a hero or have any big drums, he just wants to serve as an American. It is so hard to be in contact with him as he is at war in Iraq."

- John Michael's mother, Sylvi Hammerstrom

- PFC Soderholm, John Michael

U.S. Army
82nd Airborne paratroopers,
Army Commendation Medal recipient
Deployed Jan 27th, 2007
Currently serving in Iraq
September 11th, 2007
2ND YEAR SERVING AMERICA

# GOING TO GRANDMA LUCY'S

The huge, old, yellow bus made a whooshing sound when Mr. Benge stopped it to let me and my sisters out at Grandpa and Grandma Abernathy's. Running down the long wooded driveway with braids flying gave me time to anticipate what was soon to be ours! Every so often mom's note, sent to school, said we could go to the farm on Worthington Rd. Those days were golden; they shimmer in my mind like iridescent teardrops of joy.

## BUTTERSCOTCH SQUARES

Help yourself to Mother's brownies.

1 lb. brown sugar
1 cup butter
2 eggs
2 cups flour
1 tsp. salt
1 cup walnuts

Cook sugar and butter until it dissolves, then cool. Add eggs, one at time, beating after each. Stir in other ingredients. Bake at 350° for 25 minutes.

In my young heart, so full of expectation and promise, I held my Grandma Lucy to be queen of the kitchen. Her house was so safe and cozy, and the oven its crown. She didn't need to try lots of new fangled recipes because the familiar ones were comfortable and better than good. When Grandma Lou got on to something lip smacking, she'd stick to that certain dish over and over.

A child likes routine that works, the same predictable stories, and true blue foods. If Grandma made her special sunflower seeds 99 times, I'd ask for the 100th. Her seeds were magical. A large blackened cookie sheet, a stick of margarine, salt, several cups of raw sunflower seeds with her sweet hand to stir. Stir and roast, look over her glasses, stir and roast, bite her lips just so, stir and roast, until: Presto! Pure Bliss.

Grandma Lucy's after school treat meant the world to me. Those sunflowers seeds represented country kindness, farm kitchen come-n-get-it, served with old fashioned unconditional love. She "planted" them and made sure their "blossoms" would never stop blooming.    –Heidi Esteb

# MOUND BARS

This creation, shared by Ruth Kangas, is a favorite.

**2 cups crushed graham crackers**
**½ cup butter**
**½ cup sugar**
**1 can sweetened condensed milk**
**1 (17oz.) pkg. flaked coconut**
**8 Hershey bars**

Mix graham crackers, butter, and sugar; press into bottom of 9"x 13" pan. Bake at 350° for 10 minutes. Mix sweetened condensed milk and coconut; spread over graham cracker crust. Bake 15 more minutes, same temp., and remove from oven. Place Hershey bars over all. When Hershey bars are melted, spread like frosting. Cool and cut into bars to serve.

# CARROT BARS

Another good recipe from my sister-in-law, RuthAnn. If you car..rot all what your family thinks, these bars will be the first on your baking list.

Mix well:
**2 cups sugar**
**4 eggs**
**1¼ cup oil**
**2¼ cups flour**
**2 tsp. baking powder**
**2 tsp. baking soda**

Add:
**3 cups grated carrots**
**1 cup nuts**

Bake in a greased jelly roll pan at 350° for 35-40 minutes. Frost with cream cheese frosting.

# APPLE BARS

From Marie Rotschy.
This recipe is a big favorite!

**2½ cups flour**
**1 Tbsp. sugar**
**1 tsp. salt**
**1 cup shortening**
**1 egg yolk** (put in
    measuring cup; add
    enough milk to make
    ⅔ cup)

Roll out half of dough and
put on big cookie sheet.

Mix together and pour onto
crust:

**6 large apples (tart),**
    **peeled and sliced**
**1 Tbsp. flour**
**1 cup sugar**
**1 tsp. cinnamon**

Then roll out rest of dough
and place over the top of
apples. Beat egg whites
until frothy and brush on
top. Bake 40 minutes
at 350°.
You can glaze top of bars while
warm with:

**1 cup powdered sugar**
**1 tsp. vanilla**
**3 tsp. hot water**

# BANANA BARS

From Heidi Esteb.

1¼ cups sugar
1 cup sour cream
½ cup butter
2 eggs
3 ripe bananas, mashed
2 tsp. vanilla
2 cups flour
1 tsp. salt
1 tsp. baking soda
½ cup nuts

Mix first four ingredients in mixer for 1 minute. Beat in vanilla and bananas. Add dry ingredients and beat for 1 minute. Stir in nuts. Spread in 9"x 13" pan. Bake until light brown for 20-25 minutes at 350˚. Frost with cream cheese frosting. Sprinkle with nuts.

# CHOCOLATE SCOTCHEROOS

Jan Munger gave this yummy recipe to me years ago.

1 cup sugar
1 cup corn syrup
1 cup peanut butter
6 cups Rice Krispies
1 (6oz.) pkg. chocolate chips
1 small pkg. butterscotch chips

Cook sugar and corn syrup together until it comes to a boil; remove from heat. Stir in peanut butter. Mix in Rice Krispies. Press into 9"x 13" pan. Let harden, then melt chocolate and butterscotch chips over hot (not boiling) water; spread over mixture in pan.

# BUTTER CREAM BARS

We've been making this recipe for some time, especially at Christmas or for weddings. Juanita Reddig gave me this recipe.

⅓ cup butter, softened
¼ cup brown sugar
1 Tbsp. cream
½ tsp. vanilla
1¼ cups flour

Combine ingredients. Mix until particles are fine. Press into 9" square pan. Bake at 375˚ for 15-18 minutes, or until golden brown.

## TOPPING:
¼ cup butter, softened
¼ cup light cream
¼ cup sugar
⅛ tsp. salt
1½ to 2 cups powdered sugar
½ cup unblanched or toasted almonds
½ tsp. almond extract

Boil cream, sugar, butter, and salt together for 3 minutes. Remove from heat. Add powdered sugar until it's of spreading consistency; beat until smooth. Stir in almonds and extract. Spread over baked crust. Cool, cut into squares.

## CHERRY SQUARES

From my daughter-in-law, Debbie.

½ cup butter
1 cup sugar
1 tsp. vanilla
2 eggs
2 cups flour
1 can cherry pie filling
1 cup walnuts, chopped

Cream butter and sugar thoroughly. Add vanilla. Stir in eggs, one at a time. Mix in flour. Add nuts and mix well. Spread ¾" of thick batter into ungreased 9"x 13" pan. Cover with pie filling. Drop remaining batter by spoonfuls on filling and spread with a spatula. Bake at 350° for 35-45 minutes. Sprinkle with powdered sugar and cool.

## RASPBERRY COOKIE BARS

Really good! From Emily Peia.

1 cup butter
1 cup sugar
2 eggs
1 tsp. vanilla
2 cups flour
¾-1 can raspberry pie filling
1 cup chopped nuts

Cream eggs, butter, and sugar until light an fluffy; add flour and nuts, mixing well. Mak the dough semi-crumbly, then pat half of into 9"x 13" greased glass pan, spreading evenly with a knife. Top with raspberry p filling. Drop remaining crumbly dough mix ture on top. Bake at 350° for 1 hour or unt light brown. Cool and cut into bars. Enjoy

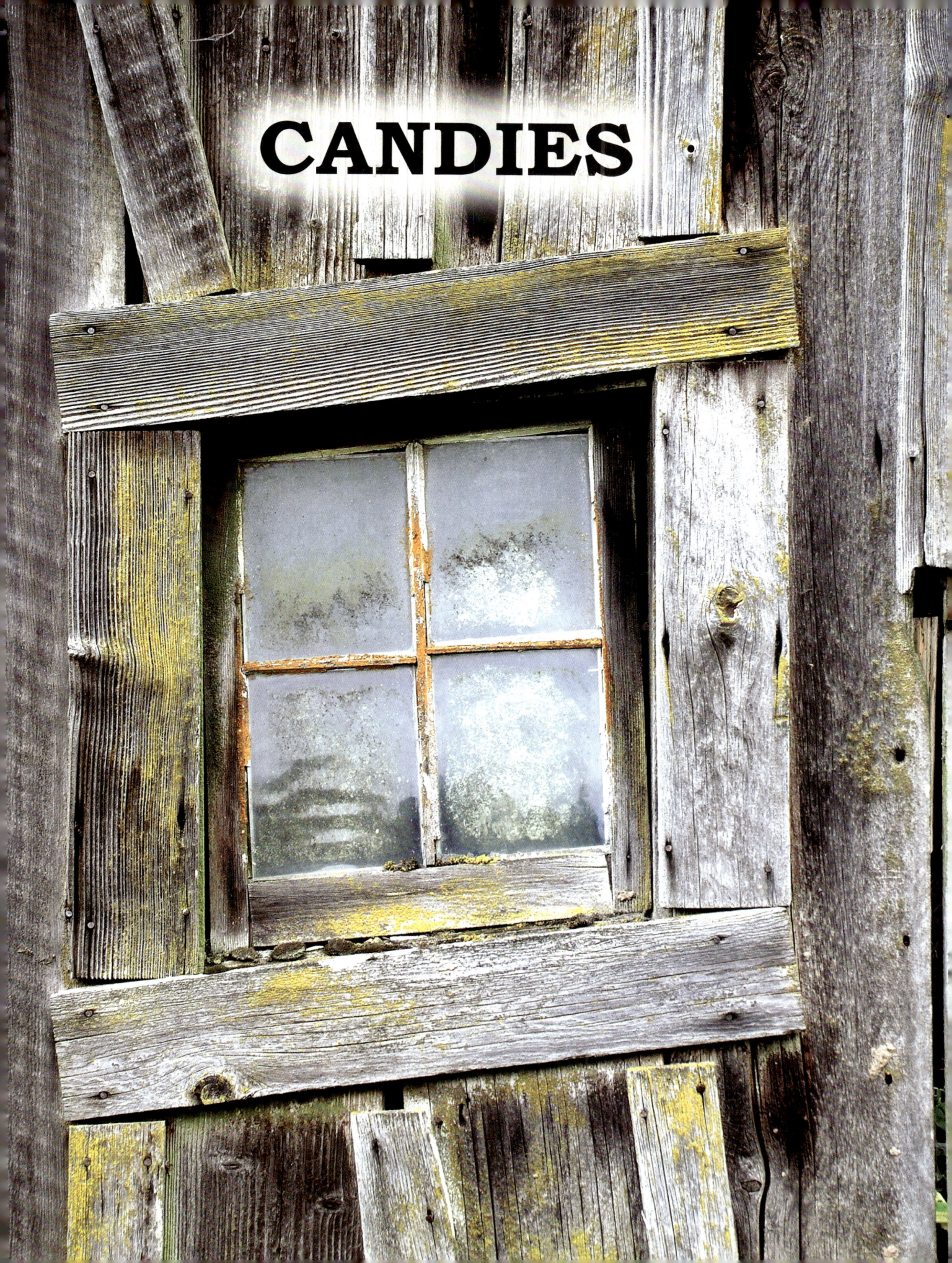

# CANDIES

# HOMEMADE NUT BRITTLE

Everyone enjoys these candied nuts!

1 cup nuts, your choice
1 cup sugar

Roast nuts in oven or microwave until lightly toasted. Put sugar in cast iron skillet. Cook over medium heat until sugar is melted and golden brown, stirring constantly. Do not break away unmelted sugar from spoon back into melted sugar. Stir in nuts and mix well. Spread onto a buttered cookie sheet. Cool. Break into pieces.

# MARSHMALLOW CANDY

A great recipe from Marlis Peters.

1 pkg. caramels
½ can of evaporated milk
1 bag large marshmallows
4 cups Rice Krispies or ground nuts

Freeze marshmallows on cookie sheet. Melt caramels with milk. Dip marshmallows into caramel mixture. Roll in Rice Krispies or nuts and drop on wax paper.

# ENGLISH TOFFEE

From Karen Rotschy. She got it from her mother and has been making it for years.

2 cups butter
2 cups sugar
2 cups almonds, coarsely chopped
6 Tbsp. water
2 Tbsp. Karo Syrup
1 tsp. vanilla
8oz. milk chocolate

Start melting butter, using a heavy pan (2qt.), over low heat. Gradually add sugar, stirring constantly. Blend in 1 cup almonds, water, and Karo Syrup. Set candy thermometer in place. Cook over medium heat, stirring a few times until it reaches 300°. (This will scorch, so watch carefully.) Remove from heat, stir in vanilla; quickly pour onto buttered cookie sheet. Cool completely. Melt chocolate over hot water (you can use microwave) and cool a little, then spread it over cooled candy. Sprinkle remaining almonds over chocolate and set aside to cool. Break into pieces and store.

# PEANUT BUTTER CUPS

Lorraine Ritola gave this recipe to me.

1 pkg. graham cracker crumbs
2 cups powdered sugar
¾ cup butter
1 cup peanut butter
1 (6oz.) bag chocolate chips

Combine all ingredients and mix thoroughly. Pat into 9"x13" pan; chill. Melt chocolate chips and spread over top of chilled peanut butter mixture. Chill until set. Cut into small bars.

# MOUNDS

I got this yummy recipe from Muzette Bobo.

½ cup butter
1 (5oz.) can canned milk
1 (14oz.) pkg. shredded coconut
1 box powdered sugar

Melt butter and mix in the rest of above ingredients. Chill overnight.
Melt:
1 tsp. paraffin wax
1 (12oz.) pkg. chocolate chips

Melt wax and chocolate in double boiler. Roll chilled mixture into balls and dip into chocolate; lay on wax paper. Chill until set.

# LEILA'S CHOCOLATE BON-BONS

This recipe is an old one, given to me by my cousin, Leila Kysar.

1 lb. powdered sugar
½ cup butter
1 tsp. vanilla
2-3 Tbsp. water

Mix thoroughly until smooth. Knead in more powdered sugar until very stiff. Roll into 1" balls and chill 24 hours on wax paper.

### (16oz.) semi-sweet chocolate squares

Melt the chocolate squares in top of double boiler (leave over hot water while dipping). Drop centers one at a time into chocolate, upside down. Turn over and lift out of chocolate with a fork. Tap off extra chocolate and push off of fork onto wax paper. Chill. May decorate if desired with walnut half on top.
I add ½ cup white chocolate chips with the butter, melted together.

# CARAMEL CORN

From RuthAnn Abernathy.

5 qts. popped corn
1 cup butter
2 cups brown sugar
2 cups almonds, whole
½ cup light corn syrup
1 tsp. salt
½ tsp. baking soda

Spread freshly popped corn in large shallow sheet pan. Put it in a very slow oven (250°) to keep warm and crisp. Combine butter, brown sugar, corn syrup, and salt in a heavy sauce pan. Boil and stir to firm ball stage (248°), about 5 minutes. Remove from heat and stir in soda. Take popped corn from oven and pour hot caramel mixture over it in a fine stream. Stir to mix well. Return to oven for 45-50 minutes, stirring every 15 minutes. Cool. Store in airtight container.

# WALNUT CARAMELS

MaryLou (Blakeman) Stewart sold these at a bazaar.

1 cup butter
1 lb. brown sugar
Dash of salt
1 cup light corn syrup
1 can sweetened condensed milk
1-2 cups walnuts

Melt butter in pan; add sugar, salt, and corn syrup. Stirring well, gradually add condensed milk. Cook and stir to 245°, add vanilla and nuts. Pour into 9"x 13" buttered pan. Cool and cut into small pieces.
I put in small pieces of wax paper and twist the ends.

# CHOCOLATE FUDGE

My mother-in-law Rose gave me this recipe before I married her son.

3 cups sugar
¾ cup cream
½ cup milk
1½ squares chocolate
1 Tbsp. cornstarch
3 Tbsp. water
1 tsp. vanilla
Pinch of salt

Put sugar, cream, and milk into pan and bring to a boil. Add chocolate and water mixed with cornstarch. Mix and stir. Cook to softball. Cool. Beat, following instructions of Caramel Fudge.

# CHOCOLATE FUDGE

Makes about 5 lbs. My mother, Lucy, made many batches of this fudge.

Put in large bowl:
3 (6oz.) pkgs. Chocolate chips
2 tsp. vanilla
2 cups walnuts, chopped
½ lb. butter
1 (8oz.) jar marshmallow creme

Put into large saucepan:
4½ cups sugar
1 can evaporated milk

Stir and bring to boil 10 minutes on low heat. Pour chocolate chip mixture into sugar and milk, and stir until chips and butter are melted. Pour into buttered pan, about 1" thick.

# CARAMEL FUDGE

Raydene McDaniels is well known for her gifts of Caramel Fudge at Christmas.

¼ cup sugar, melted
¾ cup cream
2 cups sugar
1 cup nuts, chopped

Add cream slowly to melted sugar; add 2 cups sugar and cook until a soft ball forms. Cool. Beat until it changes consistency and loses the glossy look. Add nuts quickly and pour into buttered dish. To keep this fudge from sugaring and give it a really smooth texture, I always add 1 Tbsp. cornstarch mixed in a little water when the fudge first starts to boil. If it does sugar, just add a little cream and re-cook. This is a hard recipe to master, but well worth the effort!

Mother's dark blue set of five cookbooks
called Women's Institute Library Of Cookery
was copyrighted in Great Britain. The first
three volumes were in 1918 and the last two
in 1919. The set was printed in the U.S.A. in
1925. These wonderful books came to Mother
instead of the business and secretarial books
she had ordered. The recipe for Opera Cream
calls for thin cream. Mother found that only
thick, but not lumpy cream worked. Now only
heavy whipping cream works. The book states
that the Opera Cream should be spread 1"
deep in a flat pan covered with chocolate and
cut into squares. Instead, Mother rolled the
Opera Cream into balls and dipped them in
tempered chocolate. It seems that chocolate
has varied through the years. She read in a
newspaper how to temper the chocolate in a
double boiler. Now there are other ways. We
used to put them into Christmas card
boxes to give to family and friends.
Then we changed to Christmas tins.
Everyone remembers the fantastically
wonderful smell of these candies in her
pantry at Christmas time!
-Rose Merne Gillette

# CHOCOLATE OPERA CREAMS

Grandma Rose Gillette's special candies.

**4 cups sugar**
**⅛ tsp. cream of tartar, rounded**
**2 Tbsp. white corn syrup**
**2 cups heavy whipping cream**
**Vanilla**

Mix sugar and cream of tartar; add syrup and cream. Mix well. Cook in a heavy 4-qt. stainless steel kettle, stirring with a wooden spoon until mixture comes to a boil. Do not stir after boiling has begun unless it is necessary to keep the mixture from sticking to the pan. Boil it until it registers 240° on thermometer or until a hard ball will form when ¼ tsp. is put in a cup of cold water (not ice water). The hard ball stage is reached when the ball may be rolled in the finger tips. It is not so hard, however, that an impression can not be made in it with the fingers. Pour onto a large platter which has been moistened by wiping with a cloth that has been tightly wrung from cold water. Allow to cool completely undisturbed. Mixture will be very stiff, like taffy, when cool and ready to work up. Work up cooled candy with a stainless steel table knife, until it becomes thick and creamy. We now use a high powered mixer instead of a knife to beat the candy. It loses shine and must be dull looking. Put in bowl and cover with plastic wrap. After several hours, make desired shapes using powdered sugar in hands to keep from sticking. Let stand up and dip in whatever chocolate desired.

There is something so nostalgic and so all American about a picnic, especially if the picnic is by the old fishing hole.

Farm children enjoyed this privilege when I was young!

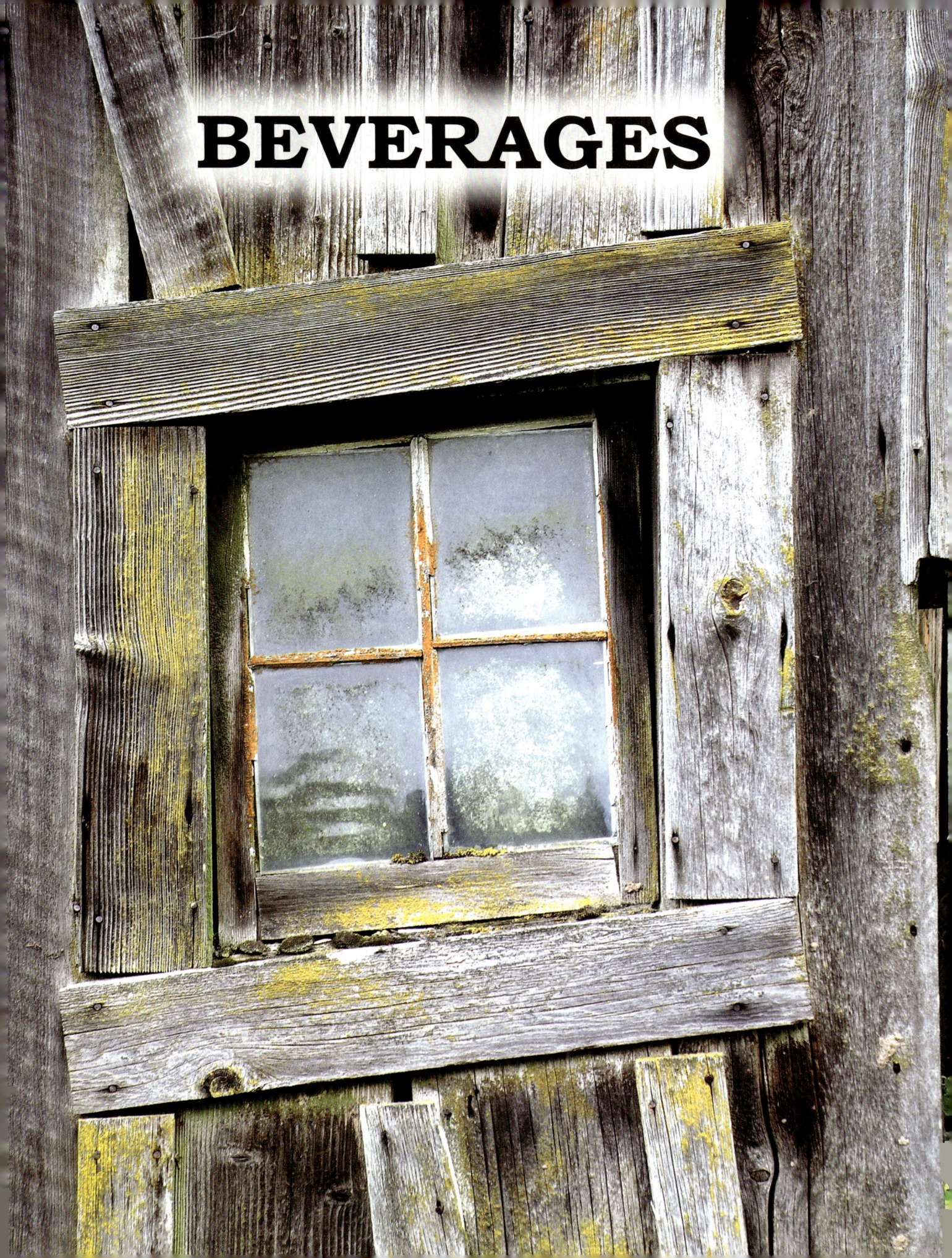

# BEVERAGES

# LEMON-Y PUNCH

Cool and refreshing!

4 qts. water
1 (6oz.) can frozen orange juice
1 (6oz.) can frozen lemonade
1 Tbsp. vanilla
1 Tbsp. almond extract
½ cup-1 cup sugar (to taste)

Make ahead of time in jumbo canister; refrigerate a few hours to let flavors blend.

# ICED TEA

A fantastic brew! From my daughter-in-law Tina. This recipe makes one gallon.

10 tea bags
4 cups boiling water
1 cup sugar
½ (12oz.) can frozen lemonade
Water

Steep tea bags for 10 minutes in boiling water. Remove bags and add sugar, stir until dissolved, then add lemonade. Fill gallon container with ice, tea mixture, and water.

# PARTY PUNCH

From my sister, Linda Kysar.

3 big cans pineapple juice
3 (12oz.) cans frozen lime juice
1 big can apricot nectar

# BANANA SLUSH PUNCH

Everyone likes this different tasty punch.

3 cups water
2 cups sugar
1 (12oz.) can frozen orange juice
1 (46oz.) can unsweetened
   pineapple juice
¼ cup lemon juice
4 bananas, pureed

Heat water and sugar until dissolved. Blend all ingredients together and freeze in four containers, approximately 3½ cups each. When ready to serve, mash with potato masher until slushy. Add 1 liter of Squirt or ginger-ale to each 3½ cup container. Total recipe serves about 40.

# STRAWBERRY LEMONADE

A great twist to lemonade!

1½ cups sugar
½ cup boiling water
1½ cups fresh lemon juice
5 cups cold water
Small carton frozen strawberries

Stir together sugar and ½ cup boiling water until sugar dissolves. Stir in lemon juice and water. Puree frozen strawberries and add to lemonade. Add ice and enjoy!

# CHOCOLATE MALTS

So delicious and old-fashioned. Can be used for a dessert with a dollop of whipped cream on top.

1½ cups milk
4 cups vanilla ice cream, softened
5-6 Tbsp. malted milk powder
1 cup chocolate ice cream topping

Combine all ingredients in milkshake maker or blender; cover and process until blended. Pour into 5 glasses. Sprinkle with grated chocolate or dollop of whipped cream.

# FRESH LEMONADE

Oh, the memories of homemade lemonade! This recipe is the way we make it today!

**6 cups water**
**1½ cups sugar**
**2 cups fresh squeezed lemon juice, about 10 lemons**
**1 can lemonade concentrate**

Make lemonade from the can, following the directions. Add the rest of the ingredients, stirring well to dissolve the sugar. Pour into glasses with plenty of ice. You may garnish pitcher or individual glasses with sliced pieces of lemon before serving. Enjoy!

# PEACH ENERGY REFRESHER

Anything peachy is great!

1 carton (8oz.) peach yogurt
1 cup milk
½ cup fresh or frozen peaches

1 Tbsp. honey
2 cups vanilla ice cream
1 banana

Place all ingredients in blender; process on high until smooth.  Pour into glasses.

# FRUIT SMOOTHIE

From my daughter, Lori Anne.   Processing the ingredients in a blender is all it takes.

1 cup juice, your choice
1 (10oz.) pkg. frozen raspberries
1 (10oz.) pkg. frozen strawberries
1 medium banana, chopped
6 ice cubes
1-2 Tbsp. sugar

Put everything but the banana in the blender. Cover and process until smooth.  Lastly, add the banana and blend to your liking.  Makes 4 glasses.

# ICED COFFEE

From Tamey Helmers, who fondly states that this delicious drink percolates from Sheridan, Wyoming.

3 cups strong fresh bean coffee
1 cup sugar
1 pint cream
1 quart milk
1 tsp. vanilla

Stir together and put in a large metal bowl. Cover.  Put in freezer several hours or overnight. Ice crystals will form on edges; scrape and stir. Serve with a smile!

# TREES

I think that I shall never see
A poem as lovely as a tree.

A tree whose hungry mouth is prest,
Against the earth's sweet flowing breast;

A tree that looks at God all day,
And lifts her leafy arms to pray;

A tree that may in summer wear
A nest of robins in her hair;

Upon whose bosom snow has lain;
Who intimately lives with rain.

Poems are made by fools like me,
But only God can make a tree.

Sergeant Joyce Kilmer
165th Infantry (69th New York)
(Born December 6, 1886, killed in
action near Ourcy, July 30th, 1918)

178

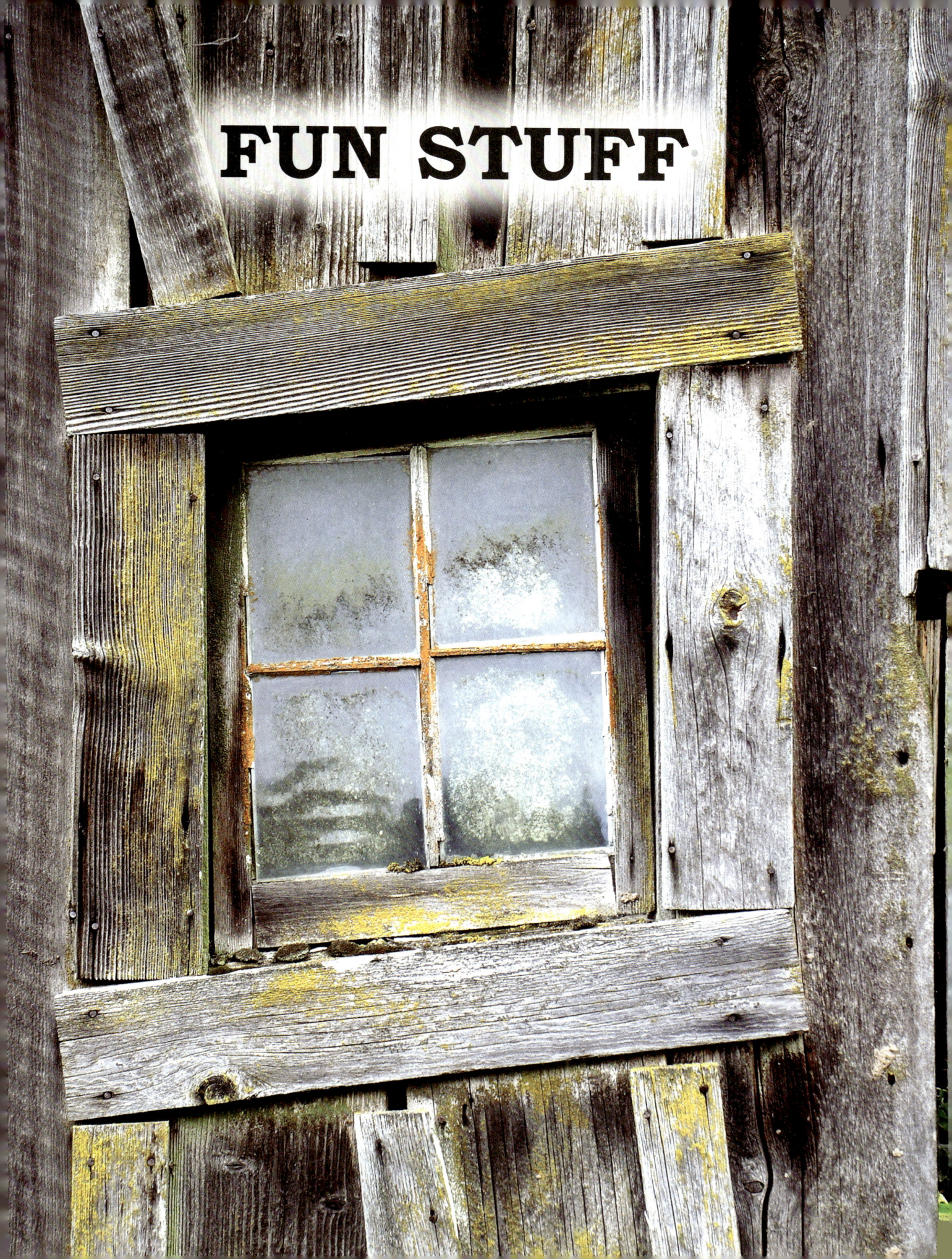

# FUN STUFF

## PICKLED BEANS

From Elaine Johnston.  Really good!

**4 pints green beans**

Place beans in jar standing upright.
Add to each jar:
**1 dried red pepper**
**1 clove garlic**
**1 head dill**

Bring to boil:
**¼ cup salt**
**2½ cups water**
**2½ cups vinegar**

Pour liquid into jars.  Put hot lids and rings
on each jar.  Process for 10 minutes.  Remove
from canner and cool.

## DILL PICKLES

Jan Prouty gave me this recipe.  I heat the brine.

**Cucumbers, washed and pricked**
**Alum**
**Dill**
**Dried red pepper**
**Garlic**
**Water**
**Vinegar**
**Pickling salt**

Into each jar, add ⅛ tsp. alum, 1 head dill, ½ tsp.
dried red pepper, and 2 slivers garlic; then pack
jars with cucumbers.  Fill to top with brine water,
1 cup vinegar, and ¼ cup pickling salt.  Cover jars
and shake to dissolve salt, if packing with cold
water.  Heat brine and lids if packing hot, pour
liquid over cucumbers and seal.

# BREAD AND BUTTER PICKLES

These crunchy pickles are very good. Recipe given by my sister-in-law, RuthAnn Abernathy.

**30-40 medium cucumbers**
**5 large onions**
**3 large green peppers**
**1 tsp. turmeric**
**1 tsp. cloves**
**2 Tbsp. mustard seed or 1 Tbsp.**
**  ground mustard**
**½ cup salt**
**5 cups sugar**
**5 cups vinegar**

Slice cucumbers; chop onions and peppers; mix together and add salt. Let stand for 3 hours with chunks of ice. Drain and rinse. Mix sugar, vinegar, and spices in sauce pan; bring to boil. Add cucumbers; simmer. Pack in hot jars and seal.

# PICKLED BEETS

The best beet pickles we've ever tasted! From my sister-in-law, Beth Malinowski.

Pour over beets in jars:
**1 cup water**
**1 cup vinegar**
**1 cup brown sugar**
**1 tsp. whole cloves**
**1 tsp. cinnamon**

Cook beets until tender. Peel in cold water. Quarter beets or use small beets. Sterilize jars and heat lids in water bath. Pack sterilized jars with beets and place jars in warm oven. Pour vinegar mixture over beets and seal. You can make as many jars as you want; double or triple vinegar liquid.

# WATERMELON RIND PICKLES

Grandmother Stanly was a master at making watermelon rind pickles. Her recipe offers this advice, "I keep mine in a wooden keg which I have waxed with paraffin. Vinegar eats into enamel if kept very long." How well I remember the hired servants serving these crisp pickles to us when we visited that big Southern mansion.

**7 lbs. watermelon rind**
**4 lbs. sugar**
**3 pints vinegar**
**1½ oz. whole cloves**
**2 sticks cinnamon** (broken)
**1½ oz. whole ginger root**
**1 Tbsp. alum**

Cut off all the soft part of rind; peel the green outside as thinly as you can. Soak in mild salt water overnight. Wash the next morning and boil 1 Tbsp. alum and water until rind is transparent; wash in about three waters, then put back on stove with the vinegar, sugar, and spices. Put the spices in a bag and tie. Then drop in the bag of spices and boil with the rind. Cook until you think they look right. Let stand in a big container for 6 weeks. Then if you wish, put in quart jars; use fresh vinegar mixture and seal when hot.

## THE BARN SWING

The old barn swing stood like a stout shadow against the evening sky. Inside the cows chewed contentedly, the day was done. The fresh smell of hay, warm milk, and grain wafted through the air. Ahhh, the smell of barn.

A gunny sack swing hung from one of the highest rafters. It stirred in the murky light and suddenly it began to move. Up, Up, Up, it trailed to a ladder nailed to the side of the barn. The rafters began to creak! Breathless chills, thrills, and rapid heartbeats; then whoosh!! Down, down, down, came the swing. Swoosh! Up it went again, flying, gliding, riding through the hay dust and shadows. Ringing laughter and clapping hands echoed and bounced off the walls. Was it a bird? Noooo. A plane? Noooo. Was it Tarzan? NO! NO! NO! It was our dear mother- the fearless one!          ~Linda Kysar

Glorious fun was had at the ole swimming hole!  The work was finished for the day,
we were all hot and tired.  No fans, no refrigerators, no air conditioners; however,
there was lots of ice cold spring water and plenty of love.  Somehow, we got to that
magical swimming hole on the Lewis River.  Sometimes we had to settle for a walk to
Cedar Creek with the crawdads.  If we were lucky, Barbara [Heidegger] Jolma took
us to Dole Valley.  Dear Mother would fix a picnic in later years, and stop at Boehm's
Store.  Watermelons were usually a dollar or less, then off to Yale Lake we'd go for a
swim and supper.  Swimming was one of summer's favorite pleasures for farm folk.

# SMOKED SALMON DIP

From daughter, Lori Anne.

1 (6.5oz.) can smoked salmon
1 (8oz.) pkg. cream cheese,
   softened
½ can water chestnuts, diced
1 Tbsp. mayonnaise

Sprinkle to taste, with the following
ingredients:
Worcestershire sauce
White pepper
Dill
Thyme
Garlic powder

Combine all ingredients and mix thoroughly
with fork until smooth. Serve with crackers
or small pieces of bread.

# SHRIMP DIP

From JoAnn Cummings. JoAnn brings this tasty
dip at holiday time; you can't stop eating it! This
dip is good with chopped clams as well as shrimp.

Put in blender:
1 small carton cottage cheese
1 small carton sour cream

Pour into and add:
2-3 cans tiny shrimp, drained
Salt and Pepper
1-2 tsp. Uncle Dan's Original
   Ranch Dressing

This dip is more flavorful if chilled for a
few hours.

# ARTICHOKE DIP

From daughter, Lori Anne.

3 cups artichoke hearts, chopped
1 cup mayonnaise
1 cup parmesan cheese, grated
2 (4oz.) cans diced green chilies
¼ cup onion, chopped (optional)

Mix all ingredients together and bake in a
baking dish at 375° for 30 minutes. Serve
warm with your favorite crackers or chips.
Can be cooked in microwave for 12-15 minutes, stirring every 5 minutes.

# SHRIMP DELIGHT

Very easy and quick, but always enjoyed!

1 (8oz.) pkg. cream cheese,
   softened
1 small jar seafood cocktail sauce
1 lb. cooked baby shrimp, rinsed
   and drained

Place cream cheese on a pretty dish. Pour
cocktail sauce over cream cheese. Place
shrimp on top and garnish with parsley.
Serve with assorted crackers.

Don't burn bridges. You'll be
surprised how many times you
have to cross the same river.

185

## ALMOND-BACON-CHEESE BAGUETTES

Be ready to serve these tasty little toasts hot from the oven.

1 baguette
4 bacon slices, cooked and crumbled
1 cup cheese, shredded
1/3 cup mayonnaise
1/3 cup almonds, sliced and toasted
1 green onion, chopped
1/4 tsp. salt
1/4 tsp. pepper

Slice baguette into 36-40 slices. Put slices on an ungreased cookie sheet. Bake at 400° for 5-6 minutes. Combine the rest of ingredients in a small bowl; stir well. Spread cheese mixture on slices. Bake at 400° for 5 minutes. Serve hot.

## PECAN CHEESE BALL

From Molly Kangas. A big hit at Christmas!

2 (8oz.) pkgs. cream cheese
1 (8oz.) can crushed pineapple, drained
1/4 cup green peppers, chopped fine
1 Tbsp. green onions, chopped fine
1 Tbsp. seasoned salt
2 cups pecans, toasted and chopped
**Maraschino cherries** (for garnish)
**Parsley** (for garnish)

Combine first five ingredients. Mix in one cup pecans. Form into a ball and wrap in saran wrap. Chill until firm. Roll in remaining pecans. Place on serving platter, garnish with parsley, pineapple, and maraschino cherries. Serve with crackers.

## BLT DIP

For all you bacon, lettuce, and tomato fans.

1/2 cup mayonnaise
1 1/2 cups sour cream
1 lb. bacon, cooked and crumbled
2 large tomatoes, chopped

Mix mayonnaise and sour cream until smooth. Add crumbled bacon and tomatoes. Serve on lettuce leaves with crackers or melba toast rounds.

## Pop Ups

One slice of Beef Salami Put On microwave safe plate Sprinkle with cheddar cheese put on microwave for 30 to One minute it will pop up like a bowl enjoy!

By Randal age 9

Lindborg

You have to love your children unselfishly. That's hard. But it's the only way.

Randal Lindberg came up to me at church about 6 months ago and asked me if I planned to do another cookbook. The next Sunday, he brought me his recipe and here it is!

Thank you, Randal, for sharing this awesome recipe.

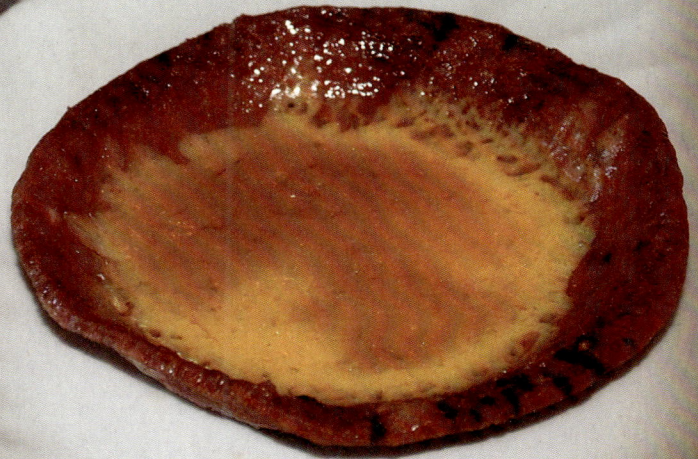

## BRITTANY'S SANDWICHES

This is begged for at Gail Kysar Schmeusser's house when her grandchildren come to visit. Gail came up with this "good ole" farm kind of treat! **Butter bread**, sprinkle with **cinnamon and sugar**, put in oven to toast, and then spread with homemade **applesauce**. Can be eaten open face or put together like a sandwich. Apple sauce can be warm or cold.

187

# BRIE CHEESE APPETIZER

From Logan and Alissa Kysar. Everyone loves this treat!

**1 prepared pie crust**
 (can use premade)

**Orange marmalade**
**Slivered almonds**
**Brie loaf**

Cover crust that is rolled out to fit a 9" pie plate with orange marmalade. Sprinkle with slivered almonds. Fold the crust around the cheese; seal it. Turn the crust (with cheese inside) over, and bake on a cookie sheet until crust is golden brown. Serve with crackers or small pieces of bread.

# CHILI DIP

From my granddaughter, Bethany Kadow. So fast and easy for company.

**2 cans chili with beef and beans**
**1 (8oz.) pkg. cream cheese**

Stir together over medium heat until hot, then serve while still warm with tortilla chips. To make it more spicy, you may use spicier chili.

# ALMOND CHEESE DELIGHT

Very good on crackers and easy to make.

**1 (8oz.) pkg. cream cheese**
**2 cups Swiss cheese, shredded**
**½ cup almonds, toasted and
 chopped**
**⅓ cup mayonnaise**
**2 green onions, chopped**
**½ tsp. pepper, freshly ground**

Mix all ingredients together and spread into a 9" pie plate. Bake uncovered at 350° for 15 minutes. Garnish with sliced almonds and serve.

# BREAD STICKS

Fast, easy, tasty, and perfect for company.
They even make your house smell yummy!

**1 pkg. yeast**
**1¼ cups warm water**
**3½ cups flour**
**½ tsp. salt**
**Butter**
**Parmesan cheese**
**Garlic salt**

Mix yeast and water together and let stand for 5 minutes. Add salt and flour, one cup at a time. After all is mixed well, knead it until smooth, then let it rise for ½ hour in bowl. Then pour dough out on flat surface with a little flour so the dough won't stick. Take rolling pin and roll dough out to ½" thick. Cut into strips. You can get fancy and twist them. Place on cookie sheet and bake at 425° for 12-15 minutes. Remove from oven and brush with butter. Sprinkle with garlic and parmesan cheese. Serve warm with your favorite sauce.

# CRUNCHY SEED BARS

**1 (16oz.) bag marshmallows**
**½ cup butter**
**2 cups flax seeds**
**1 cup sesame seeds**
**2 cups pumpkin seeds**
**1 cup sunflower seeds**
**1 cup coconut**
**2 cups almonds, roasted**
**1 cup pecans, roasted**

You can use seeds, dried fruit, and nuts of choice. Melt butter and marshmallows in a large bowl in microwave. When melted, add seeds, nuts, and co-conut. Pour into 9"x 13" buttered pan. Cut into 1"x 3" bars. So good with a cup of coffee.

Sonny and I went to Mt. Whistler for our 40th anniversary. We stopped at a Starbucks on the way up the mountain and bought a seed bar to eat with our coffee. It was so delicious and seemed nutritious. No recipe was allowed me; we were able to visit the bakery. After eating and examining five bars, I was ready to try my own hand at creating them. My version boasts of more crunch: the secret to a good nut is roasting before adding to recipe. These are addictive.

# JELL-O POKE CAKE

This is a fun and most loved cake!  I used to make it a lot, then I lost the recipe.  Now I got it again from Jeannie Nylund.

**1 box white cake mix**
**1 cup hot water**
**1 (3oz.) pkg. JELL-O—any flavor**
**1 (8oz.) pkg. Cool Whip**

Bake cake according to the directions on box. Let cool.  Poke holes over top of cake with a fork. Mix hot water and JELL-O.  Stir well and pour over cake.  Frost with cool whip and store in refrigerator for 2 hours or until serving.

# SMOOTH AND CREAMY FROSTING

This is the topping I use on JELL-O Poke Cake.

**1 (3oz.) pkg. vanilla instant pudding**
**¼ cup powdered sugar**
**1 cup cold milk**
**1 (8oz.) pkg. Cool Whip**

Beat first three ingredients until well blended. Fold into Cool Whip.  Spread onto cooled cake. Refrigerate.

# JACK'S GRANOLA

Very, very, good!  From my son-in-law Jack Uskoski.

**6 cups old fashioned oatmeal**
**1½ cups brown sugar**
**½ cup maple syrup**
**½ cup oil**
**1½ cups walnuts, chopped**
**1 cup almonds, sliced**
**1 cup coconut**

Mix brown sugar, syrup, and oil in a sauce pan. Heat until sugar dissolves.  Mix oatmeal, nuts, and coconut into a large mixing bowl.  Pour syrup mixture over dry mixture.  Spread on 2 greased cookie sheets.  Bake at 350° for 15-20 minutes, stirring and switching cookie sheets halfway through.  Let cool and enjoy.  Store in airtight container.

You can add ingredients of choice: cranberries, raisins, and other nuts.  Dried fruit should be added when pan is removed from oven.

# POTATO CAKE DOUGHNUTS

I've made these wonderful, soft doughnuts for years. Everyone loves them!

**3 eggs, beaten well**

In bowl, mix together:
**3 Tbsp. shortening**
**¾ cup sugar**

Stir in :
**1 cup mashed potatoes**

Add beaten eggs and mix well.

Sift together and add to egg mixture:
**2¾ cups flour**
**4 tsp. baking powder**
**1 tsp. salt**
**¼ tsp. cinnamon**
**Dash of nutmeg**

Chill dough and roll out to ½" thick. Cut with doughnut cutter. Let dough rest a few minutes. Fry in vegetable oil, turning doughnuts as they brown. Drain on paper towels. Serve plain, sugared, or glazed. You can play around with this recipe and make part whole wheat with buttermilk and soda.

# SOUR CREAM TWISTS

Flavorful, light and tender.

In a larger bowl put:
**½ cup warm water**
**2 pkgs. dry yeast**

After yeast dissolves, stir in:
**1½ cups sour cream**
**½ cup sugar**
**½ tsp. baking soda**
**2 tsp. salt**
**2 eggs**
**½ cup soft shortening**
**6 cups flour**

Knead dough lightly, divide in half. Roll out half into an oblong shape approximately 8 inches wide. Spread with **2 Tbsp. of butter.** Sprinkle lightly with **brown sugar and cinnamon.** Fold each section of dough in half and cut into 1" strips. Hold strips at both ends and twist. Place on greased baking sheet 2" apart. Repeat with rest of dough. Let rise for 1 hour. Bake at 375° for about 15 minutes or until golden brown. Frost with a glaze.

# ACKNOWLEDGEMENTS

Thank you to all who contributed recipes and memories. My granddaughters, Gabrielle Massie and Brooke Tormanen, along with Krista Kaski, helped me put this book together. They were willing, available, inspiring, and non-complaining; awesome and very fun to work with.

The technology part of this book was made easier by Matt and Sarah Reddig and Martel Rotschy. Thank you!

Thanks to my daughter, Heidi, who chose the title, helped to organize and compile the book and to my daughter, Lori Anne, for the inspiring words on the back cover. Gratitude goes to my daughter-in-law, Tina Gillette, for supplying the four Montana photographs.

I am ever so grateful to all who made their special recipe for photographs: Corinne Abernathy, Lucy Cahoon, Lucille Campbell, JoAnn Cummings, Cheryl Crume, Heidi Esteb, Tina Gillette, Lori Anne Homola, Molly Kangas, Corinne Kysar, Linda Kysar, Randal Lindberg, Lyudimila Palamaryuk, RuthAnn Rivers, Gail Schmeusser, Brooke Tormanen, Heather Uskoski.

I wish to aknowledge Mike Williamson and Ward Homola. They were perceptive, patient, positive, knowledgeable and very helpful.

A sincere thanks to all the proofreaders:
Corinne Abernathy, Cheryl Crume, Heidi Esteb, Debbie Gillette, Rose Merne Gillette, Sylvi Hammerstrom, Tamey Helmers, Kristina Homola, Lori Anne Homola, Janina Kerr-Bryant, Krista Kaski, Linda Kysar, Cheri Mattson, Merle Moore, Kathleen Rinta, Marilyn Rotschy, Elaine Sarkinen, Stanly and Mary Sneeden, Paula Stephenson, Judy Tikka, and Missy Williamson.

Last but not least I want to express my appreciation for all the understanding, inspiration, and help from my family. My husband is the best!

~MAY GOD BLESS YOU ALL~

# ABOUT THE AUTHOR

Frances Anna Gillette was born in Vancouver, Washington, and raised in Yacolt, Washington. Fran is the oldest of seven children and learned to cook at a very young age, when food on the farm was simple and wholesome.

Frances A. Abernathy married Francis W. Gillette in 1959; together they were blessed with eight children. Their living children from oldest to youngest, with their spouses, are: Lori & Sam Homola, Heidi & Tom Esteb, Cheri & Robin Mattson, Luke & Debbie Gillette, Mark & Tina Gillette, Cameron & Kristy Gillette, and Heather & Jack Uskoski. Their oldest son Jude died in 1969 in a car accident, a little son with curls, only three and a half years old. Three of their children live in Montana; the other four live close to their parents. For twelve years, Fran's brother, Jack, has lived with them. Sonny and Fran have forty-three grandchildren and ten great-grandchildren.

Fran, a registered nurse, and her daughter, Lori Anne, own and operate Superior Care for Seniors, Inc., a referral placement service for the elderly. Fran also does case management.

"The Old Farmhouse Kitchen" is Fran's fourth published and copyrighted cookbook. Fran printed "Tastes of Country" four times and now those books are gone. This book contains several of those treasured recipes.

Fran says, "Thank you" to all the people who have bought and used her recipe books. Her goal is to share good recipes and she feels passionate about keeping good food on the table.

The Old Farmhouse Kitchen
Corrections to Page 139
Be-Bop Rhubarb Pie
½ tsp. oil should be ½ cup oil

194